Improving Faculty Governance

❖

Cultivating Leadership and Collaboration in Decision-Making

The National Data Base on Faculty Involvement in
Governance Project

By

Michael T. Miller

Associate Professor
College of Education and Health Professons
University of Arkansas

NEW❝❞
FORUMS
Stillwater, Oklahoma
U.S.A.

NEW FORUMS PRESS INC.

Published in the United States of America
by New Forums Press, Inc.
1018 S. Lewis St.
Stillwater, OK 74074
www.newforums.com

Library of Congress Cataloging-in-Publication Data Pending

This book may be ordered in bulk quantities at discount from New Forums Press, Inc., P.O. Box 876, Stillwater, OK 74076 [Federal I.D. No. 73 1123239]. Printed in the United States of America.

International Standard Book Number: 1-58107-074-8

Cover design by Katherine Dollar.

Dedication

This book is dedicated to Lara and Patrick Miller, and to the memory of lost friends, Signe Solverson, John Allen, and Julie Liable.

Foreword

Faculty involvement in governance activities plays an important role in higher education operations. These operations have come to be reliant on shared governance activities as mechanisms for both solving structural and procedural problems, and also to create an *espirit de corps* necessary for large organizations to function efficiently. Faculty involvement, while at times slow and arduous and others quick and constructive, is a difficult, multi-dimensional issue that requires strength, sound judgment, and a thick skin to utilize effectively.

Faculty involvement takes on many shapes and forms, ranging from the traditional faculty council or senate to town-hall meetings that resemble socialist behavior. Involvement alludes to the construct of equal voices sharing in the responsibility of decision-making, outlining procedures and policy as well as the challenges that face the institution on a daily basis. Shared authority, while time consuming and often problematic in creating shared consensus, does afford the college administrator an opportunity to create a feeling of ownership and shared commitment to the issues and decisions at hand.

Faculty involvement in governance is neither easy nor smooth, regardless of who and where the involvement is attempted. Faculty are specialists, those best and brightest, who are compensated in so many different ways to provide instruction and research expertise to their appointed fields. Involvement is a task, a duty, and relies on a personal sense of responsibility to an institution. Faculty senates typically do not provide avenues to reconcile administrative and faculty disagreement; but rather, serve as a mechanism to showcase the internal disagreement of the institution.

This book is largely the result of the seven-year effort to understand and explain shared authority in higher education through the National Data Base on Faculty Involvement in Governance (NDBFIG). The NDBFIG was initiated in the spring of 1994 as a voluntary joint effort between scholars at the

University of Nebraska-Lincoln and the University of Alabama. This effort resulted in the surveying of over 5,000 faculty and the production of nearly 50 articles and conference presentations. After establishing baseline data on what faculty think about shared governance, what they think would be an ideal setting, and what their current roles are, the NDBFIG effort focused on senate leaders.

Special thanks to Thomas McCormack, retired Air Force Colonel and Provost Emeritus at Marion Military Institute in Alabama and Professor Myron Pope at the University of Oklahoma. These two individuals provided much of the direction and energy necessary for the NDBFIG's success and growth. Tom McCormack was the co-founder of the database, creating a template and plan for success. Myron Pope provided the energy and direction to bring the project into its final phases and last data collection and analyses efforts.

I am also deeply indebted to Richard Newman of Presbyterian College for his guidance, support, and direction in this research.

The following individuals provided the majority of effort for the NDBFIG, and often sacrificed their own personal time and energy to help the Data Base succeed. Those of us working with faculty involvement in governance thank these dedicated scholars: Camilla Benton, Provost, Bevill State Community College, Carl Boening, Shelton State Community College, L. Ray Brooks, President of Northwestern Technical College, Brian Garavalia formerly of Valdosta State University, James Hood of the Milwaukee Area Technical College, Kang Bai of Troy State University Dothan, James Maddox of Friends University, David Masoner of William Jennings Bryan College, Gary Miller of Biola University, Alan Seagren of the University of Nebraska-Lincoln, Stephen Vacik of Bevill State Community College, and Kathleen Randall Cramer and Carl Williams of the University of Alabama. I also thank Rose Stevenson of San Jose State University for her assistance in preparing this manuscript and her invaluable proofreading support.

Mostly, though, I thank my wife and sons, Lara, Patrick, and Peter for their support, guidance, and patience with me during the construction of this entire project.

Table of Contents

Appendices

Lists of Figures and Table

Figures

Tables

Chapter 1

The Rationale for Shared Governance

The Apacheria was not a specific land area, nor was it a highly organized brotherhood of tribes. The word represented a mystical concept, the region and union of the Apache. The imprecision was twofold: the specific territory was never defined and membership was so elastic that any Apache tribe could be included or excluded, as it preferred (James A. Michener, Texas, 1985, p. 114).

Much like the Apacheria that James Michener refers to in *Texas*, faculty senate groups are typically loosely defined, yet rigid in interpretation of the rights of involvement. Faculty groups, emphasizing specialization, at times become secondary to specific causes and issues that appeal to certain values, and the result is a loosely bound group of specialists, narrow in their academic disciplines, working to maintain their interpretation of campus community. There are literally dozens of examples of types of governance units, including representative democracies, open forums, and elected councils. The ideal concept is that the ability to make decisions that are supported structure the relationship between the administrative body and how it interacts with faculty, students, and other constituencies, that is, those being governed.

Governance is a process as well as a formal product – a process of getting things done, to be broad-based and inclusive, and to work toward consensus (key – not a promise of consensus); as a formal product, governance is an institutional characteristic that both defines an institution as well as describes an institution. Involvement, however, does not mean that faculty or staff simply make decisions. Sometimes this involvement can be in the form of recommending a course of action, recommending alternatives, or simply talking about solutions or ideas to complex problems. Indeed, some of the gravest problems arise when faculty expect to make a binding decision when in fact they are simply consulted for ideas, opinions, or options.

There are strong historical notions about the role faculty have played in shared governance activities. Some stories report small groups of faculty making reflective decisions and authoring documents such as the Yale Report of 1828. Lucas (2000) argued firmly that these quiet, collegial environs of group unanimity never existed in this historical form, an argument echoed 18 years earlier with stronger language by Baldridge (1982) who wrote that this idea was a "fable" about a "lost magic kingdom" (p. 16).

Inaccurate historical reporting, however, is not substantive enough to either defend or deny faculty involvement in governance. Contemporary colleges and universities increasingly resemble private industry, with the separation of cost centers, student as customer relations and retention, and the packaging of learning related activities into profitable enterprises. Through divisions of continuing and extension education, as well as through academic colleges, degree programs and academic content are compartmentalized and delivered through programs designed to generate revenue and meet student needs in different learning environments. The idea of college education delivery is neither purely profitable as a commodity nor isolated in an ivory tower. The results are many diverse actors and decision makers struggling for control of a curriculum and in the protection of various interests. The contemporary college campus is more akin to a complex public entity, such as a state government, more than its historically rooted monasteries. The subsequent challenge for institutions, and particularly college administrators, is how to make accurate and informed decisions for the welfare of the institution, and for faculty to take responsibility and to respond to institutional challenges. The current climate for shared decision-making is cool, perhaps somewhat pensive in regard to traditional faculty governance, at best, as management models become increasingly pervasive on campus.

The idea of making decisions for the 'welfare of an institution' is difficult to clarify and legitimate. Should institutional decisions, activities, and philosophies reflect service to a governing constituency? At what cost does this come, if any, to discipline integrity? Such questions are often dismissed by college leaders who increasingly see institutional quality tied to external indicators, such as magazine rankings, success with enrollment and grant acquisition. Indeed, the selection of quality indicators is as political a question and issue as is the notion of an academic democracy. Both are similarly bound by the attitude that neither can be denied based on a common-sense thinking, yet the intricacies of both are a prelude to the complexity of contemporary higher education.

The context of academic decision-making is the common ground where internal governance procedures and activities intersect with external bodies and behaviors, specifically intersecting externally developed policy and decision making. In its most basic form, this intersection is where boards of directors create policy or law for institutional behavior at the same time that administrators must implement these policies, and must respond to an internal body, a faculty or academic senate, that might be making alternative recommendations. The domain of the conversation has a great deal to do with the concepts of *creating for enforcement* and *recommending courses* of action. Campbell (2000) reflected on this dichotomy, suggesting that neither the external board of directors or the faculty senate had a good grasp of the realities of operating a contemporary college or university. In a tightly coupled setting, where voices and action result in a predictable reaction, the traditional and business models of decision-making certainly apply. However, in the academy where idealism and discussions of the abstract are common, even the most bureaucratic of institutions have difficulty, at best, operating on a model of consensus-driven decision-making.

What follows in this chapter, and throughout the entire text, is a critical discussion of the state of faculty involvement in governance, many of the variables that contribute to this current state of affairs, and how one national study comprised of many parts provides a strong context for discussing how to make the system better. The discussion is predicated largely on the idea that faculty members do have an inherent right to involvement in decision-making, but that a reflexive attitude toward this right will result in their being largely manipulated by even the most well-intentioned administrator. Democracy in academic environments, as elsewhere, is reliant on the individual's ability to speak out and be heard and to have a say in how things are done. Yet, as in all democratic communities, this voice and action is only as strong as the individuals are willing to make it.

State of Decision-Making in Colleges and Universities

Decision-making on the college campus has increasingly been likened to that of business and industry. In addition to the rise of administrative personnel positions, the separation of the college into different costing categories represents a different mind set about the work of the university. Ancillary enterprises now often dominate conversations about the university as they produce substantial revenue for the college. Patent and trademark representation, research, development, and technology parks, money-making athletic programs, and contract training are all areas of the university that generate a great deal of publicity while also generating institutional income. To a large extent, these activities have increasingly come to overshadow the intricacies of the college curriculum and faculty work.

From an administrative perspective, change and adaptation in service and resource provision plays an increasing role for the university, while faculty resistance to "quick-turn around" and continual curriculum adaptation to meet learner-customer needs has increased. Although not universal resistance, there is a growing feeling that institutional decision-making neglects faculty, and de facto, curricular interests. This corporatization of the university is receiving increasing attention.

The work of colleges and universities continues to be segmented on various organizational behavior forms, such as those models offered by Birnbaum (1988), including the structures of collegial, bureaucratic, anarchical, and hierarchical decision-making. Nelson and Watt (2000) have argued that colleges and universities increasingly resemble the bureaucratic model where specific administrators and managers are hired to work in very specific and narrow areas of responsibility. Aronowitz (2000) similarly argued that the university has become a corporate entity, with the demise of attention to learning and more emphasis and overall attention on such revenue generation as soft-drink sponsorships, out-sourcing bookstores, and the dramatic increases in hiring part-time faculty.

On-campus decision-making and problem solving is accomplished to advance the best interests and mission of the college or university. The disconnection between administration and faculty subsequently arises from the sometimes conflicting visions of the institution. Additionally, there continue to be questions of trust between the ability and responsiveness of faculty to take on programs of work and solve problems in a timely and meaningful fashion, and the administration, who are often seen to be working for personal advancement and glory. Although no singular perspective will escape conflict, faculty trust of administrators and vice versa is a topic in desperate need of attention. With the movement of administrators to a more managerial casting, it is doubtful that this will change anytime in the near future.

The context for decision-making is a combination of inefficiency, blurred authority and purpose, and nearly indescribable relationships with various campus offices. College presidents typically recognize the need for faculty governance units, but the power they invest in these bodies ranges widely. Also, as seen in the study reported later about college presidential views of faculty senates, this relationship may look appropriate and wise politically, but can be viewed as dysfunctional and undesirable.

The context for shared governance is also a combination of group world-view (how those affected see things) and access to power (an ability to control or access control of resources). The over-arching concern, though, has more to do with interpretations of decision-making relevant data. Administrators, who must respond to constituent needs in a visible manner and who have professional careers that are tied to annual evaluations tend to see campus activities, events, and data in a particular light. This light tends to see the college enterprise as a business, and not particularly a nonprofit business. With the broadening of institutional portfolios to include customized and contract training, community service, small business development, and among other activities, patent and copyright development management, traditional education for degree attainment has become less of a central facet of institutional behavior. This shifting of institutional focus reflects the world-view of career administrators who tie success to indicators such as investment returns, facilities renovation, and the like.

For faculty members, employment does carry evaluation in the form of teaching evaluations, although these are rarely an adequate fuel by themselves for termination. Similarly, annual faculty evaluations by department chairs or deans rarely are seen as employment threatening. What faculty do have is progress toward tenure. Faculty termination typically comes in relation to progress toward tenure or in a tenure decision. With a faculty career generally spanning multiple decades, the tenure decision carries a great deal of weight. Indeed, once promoted from assistant to associate professor, often with the granting of tenure, the only other level of promotion eligible for faculty is from associate to full professor (Shapiro, 2001). The result in the context of decision-making is an insulation by faculty to defend a system of protected-employment and resentment by administrators toward the protected classification. The resentment can further build as faculty see better paid, mobile, and advancing administrators trek through institutions while they remain a relatively unchanged body.

Governance conceptually has a relationship with the notion of power on campus, and who or what parties or individuals have a right or ability to be involved in the conversations that drive the institution. The conversations can be vital to the institution, such as where resources should be, to the mundane, debating the problems of the daily operation of the institution. Frequently faculty are of the opinion that they are entitled to be participants in the conversation; that they have an academic right to involvement, and often, that their collective voices should offer the final word on select issues. At other times, faculty see the administration of the institution as the responsibility of paid administrators who can reflect on issues on a daily basis. No clear line to discern who is responsible for different issues has been drawn, as the result, on a national level, is a wide variety of interpretations of how faculty can and should be involved.

The current program of research accepted a "ladder" approach to faculty involvement in governance, where in a hierarchical fashion, levels of authority and responsibility are assumed by faculty governance units. Based on the conceptualization of Arnstein (1976) and Murphy (1991), faculty members are involved in different levels of governance, and their actions have distinctly different consequences, results, and meanings. Arnstein developed the framework in the context of citizen participation in school management, and to varying extents, parents and the citizenry can collaborate and have responsibility delegated to them by school authorities. Similarly, faculty involvement contends that faculty members serve as a form of citizenry, and that they, too, can have a voice in institutional decision-making. The framework holds that faculty governance units are designed to have different outcomes, based often on either the authority granted to them by administrators or the authority assumed by the governance unit, often through experience and a case of tradition.

The ladder consists of eight distinct "rungs," clustered into three categories of involvement: non-participation, tokenism, and faculty power (Figure 1). The first set of "rungs" in non-participation include governance activities, individuals, and units that perform at levels of (1) manipulation and (2) therapy. The second set, those of token involvement, include (3) informing, (4) consultation, and (5) placation. Gilmour's (1991) work, as well as the American Association of University Professors (AAUP) study of 1966 found consultation to be the primary form of practiced governance. The third set, those of faculty empowerment, include (6) partnership, (7) delegated power, and (8) faculty control. Although Baldridge (1982), Kerr (1991), and others have effectively argued that true faculty governance has never been in place, accepting the notion of Williams, Gore, Broches, and Lostoski (1987), ideal situational governance may well be in practice in some institutions, and in many institutions depending upon the issue being addressed.

Figure 1
Ladder of Faculty Involvement in Governance

8	Faculty Control	
7	Delegated Power	Degrees of Faculty Power
6	Partnership	

5	Placation	
4	Consultation	Degrees of Tokenism
3	Informing	

2	Therapy	Degrees of Non-Participation
1	Manipulation	

Increasingly on the college campus, the college president plays the role of setting the overall institutional agenda. This agenda, often bartered between the presidential candidate and the selection committee or board of trustees, can be resistant to the evolutionary state of the campus. Rosovsky (1990) noted this phenomenon, as did Bergmann (1991) and others who have claimed that presidential leadership often runs contrary to faculty depictions of organizational evolution. As the faculty, a disparate group of constituents, responds to issues, the president or provost assumes a position of control or manipulation over faculty through formal and informal power relationships.

Birnbaum (1988) described different visions of presidential leadership where the position, as much as the person holding the position, relates to faculty and others from a position of manipulation. Much like a "godfather," the institution's president works to control the agenda of the faculty governance unit through intimidation, manipulation, coercion, and office based power. In some instances, the president's position relies on charismatic leadership to engage faculty constituents, and in others, office based power is the strategy of choice. Regardless of where the president draws power, the intent of the relationship in this model between the president and the faculty governance unit is one of manipulation and control beyond the normal workings of a traditional political model.

Context of the Faculty Member

The college faculty member undertakes a number of different roles and assumes a variety of responsibilities, ranging from the most basic teaching, research, and service, to leading teams of faculty, administrators, and staff through evaluation efforts, coordinating work assignments for entire departments and programs, and coordinating technology infrastructure. Faculty members are professionals, although sometimes not seen as such, who provide key services in providing an environment or culture of learning. Traditionally educated through a graduate school experience that leads to a terminal degree, most faculty members are not taught to undertake work outside of the skills directly in line with their discipline areas, such as chemistry experimentation, statistical work, and various forms of evaluation and testing. The result is a professorate comprised of specialists in their content areas with few formal teaching skills, and the result on most college campuses is a faculty who is collectively challenged by the art of teaching and advising.

Despite a general concern about teaching and instructional quality, discussions of graduate school training often highlight a lack of teaching training, particularly in the hard sciences. This lack of functional training about how to be a teacher only begins to be indicative of the lack of formal skill training in the citizenship of the academy. What does it mean to be a faculty member? What expectations are formalized through appointments and contracts, and what sub-textual expectations are implied through a faculty appointment? What rights are delegated to faculty members in the domain of the curriculum and in the domain of administration or governance?

These types of issues reflect a duality of thinking about the context of faculty members. First, college faculty members are expected to be good teachers, performing with the best interests of students in mind, providing current and historical contexts for subject matter competence. They are subsequently given some reward for this good teaching, and colleges and universities even recognize this through institutional teaching awards. Second, though, professional recognition and esteem is generally developed through research excellence. Research productivity, while tangible in the form of articles, books, and presentations, is transferable across institutions and is publicly visible. Teaching excellence, however, can vary widely between institutions, and issues such as teaching load, undergraduate as compared to graduate instruction, topics, and student preparedness can all dramatically impact a teaching experience. The duality of the thinking is in relation to what faculty members are taught to do and what they are expected to do, and what the institution and profession will reward. The broadly interpreted result is that faculty members aggressively publish, maintain some institutionally-defined notion of decent teaching, work in service that is correlated with either a discipline, a personal value, or a department, and that after the awarding of tenure the faculty member's performance declines.

How faculty members internalize this behavior expectation and what they do with it differs dramatically. Largely, though, the newer generation of faculty on campus recognize they have a need to be involved in all three pillars of the academy, yet research productivity *vis a vis* publication is the dominant activity. To the extent that work life issues are prevalent, engagement in service in the form of governance can become important, although existing infrastructures to engage faculty involvement in governance are limited at best.

At least some mention should be made of the significant differences between the corps of faculty working at community, junior, and technical colleges as compared to their four-year university counterparts. Parenthetically, there are significant differences in both the structural operation and internal workings of community and technical colleges, and this may be highly important in later conversations dealing with how faculty see their role and what types of responsibilities they may have. In general terms, technical and vocational colleges are tightly coupled with their local communities and make concentrated efforts to supply job-trained labor for local markets. Although they do enter into broader, community education activities, their primary actions are focused on preparing a workforce.

In contrast, community colleges tend to be larger institutions in scope, assuming some workforce preparation and development certificate programs along with general education type streams of study that can be transferable to four-year institutions. Community colleges derive their mission from the idea of community service, often providing extensive community education programs in the arts, recreation, hobbies, leisure studies, and even the traditional liberal arts.

Many states have adopted legislation that requires the general education core curriculum of a given state to be consistent and transferable among institutions, meaning that community colleges can legally be seen as feeder institutions. The attractiveness of this type of programming for students is obvious and includes often lower tuition, an opportunity to remain at home or at least in a hometown while completing general education, lower student-to-faculty ratios, an easier transition either from a high school or in a return to formal education, and time for students to make academic major decisions. In funding-formula states where enrollment is tied directly to allocations, this type of arrangement can greatly favor academic transfer as these courses are typically less expensive to operate with large numbers of students and allow for greater enrollments than do highly specialized vocational training.

These types of issues surround the community college faculty member at a time of tremendous change and growth. As the contemporary community college movement is relatively young, the initial generation of faculty members who were employed by community colleges are beginning or already have retired. This founding workforce was recruited from high school teaching ranks, and the result was often a highly personalized experience where community college faculty were rewarded for their excellence in teaching. As this generation is replaced, a fundamental shift might be identified among the new ranks of faculty.

Few in the literature base have attempted to profile any major shifts in thinking about the community college reward structure, although Laabs (1987) highlighted a trend he observed. He found that reward structures in community colleges often favored those with advanced degrees, namely, doctoral degrees. And as community college faculty return to or begin advanced study, often with a research focus, they begin to see an alternative to teaching excellence as a reward. The idea has not been fully embraced within the community college community, but the seeds for Laab's predictions are certainly present.

The current community college faculty are an eclectic group of scholars and practitioners with broad ranges of experience and education. Many occupational fields of study maintain professional work experience as a dominant requirement and include some education beyond a high school diploma or associate's degree. In the liberal arts, the community college has become a primary employment objective for new faculty who see the institution as an entry to the profession and a first step on the pathway to a four-year institution, and increasingly, a destination employment. The notion of destination employment radically alters the composition of community college faculty as these faculty members target teaching at a particular level of institution and intend on remaining. Often coming from the most respected graduate schools and programs, these individuals see such environments as rewarding and meaningful without the demands of research or the discipline issues of secondary school.

Community colleges also make use of individuals with impressive professional experience, and continue their tradition of looking to community and state leaders as institutional administrators. With a history in the public or private sector, new faculty members can approach the community college with much less reverence for traditions seen as impediments to progress.

Most colleges that make use of faculty senates and councils do so on a representative democracy basis, meaning faculty from a school, college, or department are expected to represent the issues, concerns, and voices of their colleagues to the larger institution, report back to their "constituents," and serve as a trusted delegate. The infrastructure in place for the past three or four decades does not recognize a value or the importance of this representative thinking, instead encouraging individualistic behavior with little regard to gaining input and feedback from colleagues.

The issue of value of involvement subsequently becomes

doubly impaired due to the lack of collegial response to involvement along with tenure and promotion guidelines that certainly recognize the importance of involvement, yet give it relatively little weight. If faculty members are not encouraged to engage their colleagues in representation and if senior colleagues expect a quiet pattern of representative behavior, the real value of involvement to the faculty member is substantially diminished. A further result of this decreased value is thinking about shared governance in terms outside of representative democracy, perhaps something more akin to customer or citizen thinking, with responsibility placed on individuals to voice concerns and issues for clarification, action, or "service," rather than relying on established bodies to carry the will of the campus citizenship.

The culture of faculty also has a *de facto* element of aggressiveness and ambition. Participation in public debates, presentations at annual meetings, election to positions of importance in professional associations, and perhaps some publication, editorial writing, and speaking all provide for reputation development. The notion of reputation development has a great deal to do with internal motivation, perhaps relating to one of many batteries of personal work motivation, such as Maehr and Braskamp's (1986) personal investment theory that includes accomplishment, affiliation, achievement, and power as the four primary motivations for work behavior. Accepting some truth in the notion of faculty ambition, campus involvement also can play a role in faculty motivation through appealing to a desire for affiliation. As Westerfield (personal communication, 1997) has alluded, service on institutional faculty governance senates provides exposure to a broad base of issues and individuals, and allows for experience in making decisions that impact a wide range of constituents. In essence, faculty involvement in governance can be seen as a means of leadership development within the academy. Trow (1990) has gone to great lengths to contend this, noting the value of faculty governance has to do with protecting the integrity of the curriculum and academic ideals; however, a variety of case studies suggests that faculty do indeed see service as a means for professional leadership development and to create opportunities for career advancement in non-faculty ranks.

Democracy and Demand Making

The process of sharing authority in higher education has often been viewed in terms of democratic responsiveness to "citizen needs." Citizens can be any number of constituents, including students, faculty, staff, the local community, and consumers of research and knowledge produced by faculty. Universities, then, can be likened to cities or urban centers, as they provide an array of services to citizen-consumers. And, even though the constituencies identified above may have an interest in the actions of the university or college, that interest and the subsequent demand (at different levels) for action or service does not necessarily reflect a willingness to pay by the consumers.

Demands can differ, and refer to the variety of ways in which citizens (students, faculty, staff, alumni) register their preference for the delivery of a particular service at a particular time and place for a charge. Service delivery, whether in curriculum responsiveness, providing opportunities or cultural events, and so forth, is typically keyed to demands and the intensity of these demands. This suggests a natural conflict, but that does not necessarily mean there is an adversarial relationship between the campus citizens and decision-makers. Citizen-initiated contacts with faculty senators and administrators is a much more routine, invisible activity, geared toward matters of everyday service delivery rather than large-scale policy issues. Aaron Widalsvky (1988) identified this concept as the Adam Smith rule that states "when a customer makes a request, take care of that client in a professional manner; otherwise leave him alone."

The foundation of citizen-demand making as a political form of decision-making and activity for an organization is grounded on the principles that:

- Citizens initiate contact making
- Political operations are based on individualistic efforts
- Residents move or change neighborhoods or districts as a reaction to not having demands met, and
- Mobility is the exit option and exit options are about economics. The alternative of the mobility option is a vocal option, which is really about political behavior.

Citizen demand making can be viewed on a college campus as sharing many similarities with the general public, with the primary difference that shared governance bodies replace other forms of elected representation. Instead of citizens living in neighborhoods and suburbs, faculty and students vote in elections. Student "mobility" is converted to whether or not they enroll in a particular institution or if they leave; faculty "mobility" has more to do with whether appointed faculty stay in their jobs or move to other institutions.

Often, faculty governance units are required to initiate contact with various campus offices, and must pressure these offices to review, consider, accept or respond to their agendas. Similarly, faculty members, those intelligent and highly trained specialists, undertake their actions as individuals with separate agendas rather than as tightly coupled bodies.

The analogy of a campus community and citizen demand making is particularly relevant when considering the loosely coupled nature of shared authority on a college campus and the relationship between faculty and administration. Miller and Seagren (1993) identified one of the greatest barriers to effective faculty involvement in governance as the lack of trust between administrators and faculty. This notion of trust had been introduced two decades earlier (McConnell & Mortimer, 1971; Mortimer, 1974), and remains an issue of conflict and a destructive variable in shared decision making.

Citizen demand making is also relevant as a decision-making model in the university setting when considering Aronowitz's (2000) arguments relating to the corporatization of the college community. In Aronowitz's examination of the contemporary college, much attention is directed not at intellectual cultivation, but the development of revenue centers and activities that can increase positive cash flow.

Power and Resources for Decision-Making

Campus politics in virtually every sense have been or can be related to Howard Bowen's (1980) laws of higher education finance, which include:

(1) The dominant goals of institutions are educational excellence, prestige, and influence.

(2) In quest of excellence, prestige, and influence, there is virtually no limit to the amount of money an institution could spend for seemingly fruitful educational ends.

(3) Each institution raises all the money it can.

(4) Each institution spends all it raises.

(5) The cumulative effect of the preceding four laws is toward ever increasing expenditure (pp. 19-20).

This search for prestige and influence has been most recently evidenced in such rankings as the *U. S. News and World Report* annual rankings of colleges and universities, which despite innocuous claims of innocence, have become a major issue in college operations. Institutions desire to be well respected and admired, and are willing to invest strategically to be considered in a top tier, with little regard for student learning and happiness. Resources rather than student learning, apparently, are the motivations for determining institutional stature. The ways in which institutions invest these resources, though, have the potential to foster institutional internal behaviors that can indeed enhance student learning and welfare.

Authority, as a management concept, has roots in the control and formal power assigned to an individual or particular office. French and Raven (1959) have specifically broken down the various types of power, but in the practical and pragmatic world of management, individuals are assigned tasks, and are (or are not) given the authority (right) to accomplish these tasks. The mere idea of a management "right" can create hostility, particularly in the college setting where a certain level of collegial behavior is assumed. From a legal perspective, there are specific assignments made to a job, and an institution, through its structure and board of trustees or directors, and these bodies assign the power to undertake specific tasks. Through this assignment, a legal precedent is exercised, and that relies on a formal board to determine, ultimately, who has responsibility for various tasks.

The sharing of authority is reliant on a formal or implied relationship that allows access to authority. The legal restriction to the sharing of authority is primarily limited to bargaining units, and any granting of power is reliant on a board to grant such requests. Authority, then, is an ability as well as an assigned right, regulated by a legal body for the purpose of accomplishing the tasks and goals of the organization or agency. If authority is a form of responsibility, governance must, by definition, be some form of an extension or a body of activities that enable agency or organization work to be accomplished. Governance is an activity that enables a process focused on the policy and work required of an organization. Distinctly different from administration, the concept of governance has a relation to policy and methods of work to be accomplished. Governance is a distinct process, condoned by a governing board, and granted, *de facto*, at least some form of legal representation. By extension, governance implies a system or method, and typically refers to a structure as well as a process for undertaking a program (or lack of) of work.

The concept of faculty governance, then, implies some form of vested authority completed through a structure and process of governance. Faculty governance is an implied part of the collegium, the structure perpetuated in higher education based on faculty characteristics and rights. The "collegium" refers to a shared value system and collectively agreed upon set of values, beliefs, and mores that enables an environment of intellectual development and community to be fostered and developed in a meaningful manner that advances an intellectual discipline or specialization.

A residual component of the authority and governance conversation may be thematic of academic democracy. Few would advocate a pure democracy with one person one vote on all matters related to administration; however, the intellectual freedom of the college may well suggest, at the very least, forums to hear, respect, and explore different voices, mind sets, and belief systems. Therefore, democracy, as a form of political organization and social order, may well have strong roots on the college campus where representative democracy may be an expected and future norm for institutional behavior.

The relative complexity of the authority and governance, perhaps continuum, necessitates the critical discussion of how governance occurs on campus, and what those involved in the process understand and foresee as expectations and foundational behaviors. Governance, further complicated through regional accrediting body requirements, requires a broad based, inclusive approach to decision-making.

This inclusiveness is problematic, at best, as the process rarely resembles the tightly coupled models of private sector enterprises. A primary difficulty is that the participants in the process often have different perspectives and motivations from others in the organization. With highly specialized and trained scholars with a high degree of compartmentalization, faculty members expect vastly different things from the governance process. The entire experience, then, resembles a challenging method for decision-making and problem solving for the organization and its leaders, resulting in a real need for a critical, constructive conversation about how to share responsibility, authority, and ultimately, governance in higher education.

The nature, and perhaps the context of shared governance is both ambiguous, yet at times, specific. Ambiguity is drawn from the history of loose coupling and expectation, yet this very expectation also feeds the ideology of taking action and expecting action based on commentary. This contradiction feeds the need for constructive dialogue about not only how to make decisions and formulate policy that is broad based and inclusive, but how to do it well and in a meaningful fashion.

Benefits and Barriers

Sharing governance can be the result of actions and authority granted or given, and despite the expansive difference, is often motivated by one of two general schools of thought. These frameworks for establishing or utilizing shared governance, primarily with faculty, are exercised largely through presidential direction as an established "matter of course," and more than likely, as a preemptive defensive mechanism to group policy and action in the daily life of the campus.

This somewhat cynical perspective on encouraging faculty involvement in governance is directly linked to the first school of thought, being a positive relationship developed on campus. By encouraging faculty to participate in governance, new and diverse ways of thinking about complex problems can be generated, and by allowing access to the decision-making process, increasing feelings of ownership. Evans (1999) outlined a host of positive impacts sharing governance can have on an institution, including:

- improved or enhanced morale
- more creative policy formation
- grass roots support for decisions and policy
- greater buy-in for difficult situation solutions
- more support and effort by faculty to accomplish the work identified

These ideas are not necessarily new and have been identified frequently in management literature (Miles, 1965). The notion of their use and effectiveness in higher education, however, is relatively unexplored with a great deal of speculation and assumption present in this use as a motivation for supporting faculty co-governance. Many of these ideas have been supporting tools in the Total Quality Management (TQM) initiatives that have been popular on college campuses recently, and all function on the most basic concept of empowering workers to create better production.

The idea is not always embraced, as evidenced by some private sector businesses that have attempted to utilize a team-based philosophy. These businesses have found that workers do not always embrace taking on more responsibility, particularly when managers are employed to accomplish the same tasks. A car manufacturer, for example, boasted of "empowering" frontline workers with the ability to stop production if they noticed a deficiency in a car as it moved down the assembly line. In this environment, workers could protest (a) the responsibility for the total car quality when many different individuals are employed to build it, (b) the idea that equal peers are suddenly evaluating each other's work quality, (c) the fiscal cost of stopping an entire assembly line when the extent of the rationale is unknown, and (d) professional quality managers' efforts being interpreted as "pushed down" to the least compensated.

The argument, as implied, works in both directions, as frontline workers in any business are usually the first to notice quality problems. For colleges and universities, though, it is a difficult problem because there are many different levels of frontline workers, and those on the academic assembly line have little interest, and often little expertise, in the overall governance of the institution.

Why Faculty are Involved

As alluded to earlier, faculty are involved in governance activities for a variety of reasons and in the hopes of fulfilling a variety of agendas. Williams, Gore, Broches, and Lostoski (1987) have provided one of the strongest arguments for faculty involvement, finding that a combination of age, career status and ambition, and topic all correlate to produce different levels of involvement to noninvolvement. This type of thinking, indeed, reflects the complexity of motivations and incentives for faculty involvement, taking different dimensions of work life into consideration. The central tenet to their argument, however, was that the value an individual assigns to an issue or topic drives a faculty member's level of involvement. Therefore, issues that relate closely to the belief and value system of a faculty member will result in heightened levels of action and activity.

Little scholarly attention within the past two decades has been focused on political values and involvement of faculty, perhaps abandoning the personal passion argument that served as a major component of the machinery that drove the academic freedom movement of the late 1960s. So while faculty are truly becoming a managed profession, a concept reinforced by the substantial growth of unionization, higher education administration has become much more of a career, and as a result, administrative behavior has gone from being faculty-focused to institutionally-focused. The institution, in a sense, has matured, but embraced motives that are more self-serving and preservation oriented, both ideas advanced by Kerr (1991). The administrative rise and professionalization of administrative ranks provided the impetus for Bergman (1991) to refer to higher education as consisting of a "bloated administration and blighted campuses" (p. 12).

The involvement of faculty in shared governance processes

has more to do with perceptions about life and work style. Although the Gore and Williams team certainly have valid and meaningful findings, the majority of topics addressed in any given academic year do not respond to the core set of values of a faculty member. Indeed, most topics addressed by faculty senates and councils have more to do with the mundane, administrative-type issues that can have a long-term impact on institutional culture but have little immediacy in the public eye. Topics such as by-law revisions may inspire a few faculty members to get up in arms, but for the majority, these types of issues take on a certain placidity that can encourage faculty apathy.

The central question, to be addressed and examined is why faculty choose to be involved in the absence of a burning issue or topic, and why faculty members voluntarily participate in governance activities that may never deal with issues or topics that appeal or get at the core set of beliefs and values of a faculty member. Why do faculty members get involved in faculty senates in the first place, and what keeps them coming back to meeting after meeting? Why do faculty members get involved in activities that have no apparent or immediate reward? Why do faculty members get elected to positions that require the scrutiny of examination by their peers? The answers are all multifaceted and often extremely individual.

In general faculty choose their profession either as a calling or as a vocation, and for a lucky few, their avocation is indeed their vocation. The faculty lifestyle, however, carries with it a strong sense of autonomy and a reward structure that often praises longevity rather than specific successful activities. Faculty have been described as misfits who can only fit in on a college campus, where extreme diversity and differences are applauded and gratefully accepted. In such a scenario, one driving force for accepting responsibility in governance activities must be out of gratitude and social responsibility. Some faculty members are simply so excited about the lifestyle and so grateful to be a part of the academy, they altruistically give back to their host environment. In a sense, these are "do-gooders" who typify the positive citizenship attributes that are often idealized in political science literature. Similarly, there are also those faculty members who are committed to the ideals of a democratic environment and see involvement as an activity of responsibility.

Most faculty, however, have academic passions that run much deeper than institutional affiliation, a trend also observed in the notion of the gypsy-scholar who commits to a discipline for a lifetime rather than an institution. Caesar (2000) noted a hybrid approach to the gypsy-scholar and academic cosmopolitan. A theme Cesear held in *Traveling Through the Boondocks* was that the discipline provides the entry-way to professorate, but the quality of that academic experience is based on a number of variables such as where a scholar publishes, which meetings are attended on an annual basis, nature of research, and somewhere down the list, teaching performance.

Impact on Faculty Involvement in Governance

In addressing the basic question of how faculty involvement in governance works and how well it works, the background is certainly not neatly aligned along hierarchal authority. Allusions to power and prominence, discipline and institutional reputation all couple with personal motivation and administrative behavior to result in basic questions about how to share power. Indeed, the challenges facing colleges and universities in this regard are no different from those of other organizations who have high levels of ambiguity and rely on human capital for output. Organizational behavior is reliant on communication and defining expectations. From this level of understanding, the notion of who can do certain tasks and make certain decisions can be clarified, but the predominant issue must be the delineation of responsibilities and expectations.

The basic problem in this delineation is simply that those with the power have historically made these decisions and have basically enforced them on bodies of faculty with instructions. In some cases there are exceptions to this, but generally faculty senates and councils perform tasks at the behest of administrators. Administrators are, in turn, regulated, monitored, and at times manipulated by boards of trustees who can at times see personal or political agendas as preferential to institutional performance. All of this, of course, is done with the supposed best interests of faculty, students, and citizens in mind, but in fact, quite the opposite can be the norm (Campbell, 2000).

A general secondary problem facing faculty senates is the question of expectations. Few senates or governance bodies have clear assessment measures of success, and rely on personal reports of whether it was a "good" or "bad" year for the senate. With such subjective evidence of performance, broad questions of whether the governance body addressed faculty and institutional needs can fall by the wayside, and once again, personal agendas become dominant. This calls to question the motivation for involvement and participation of faculty members at all types of institutions. Are the best interests of the collective body brought to the senate agenda, or do special interest groups and action committees or teams, or administrative or trustee agendas dominant activities? Why do these items get attention when the other needs of the campus are neglected? Such questions certainly presuppose a rational decision-making process and set of motivational assumptions about involvement. The result, though, is a highly political process where those in public service are brought closely in line with the academy. In many instances this is consistent with public service perspectives, yet, faculty are also quick to note the pure and basic ideals of academic life outside of the public sphere.

As the higher education industry continues to evolve, there is a clear dominance of relevance and "students-as-customers" thinking. The ideals of an ivory tower continue in few isolated instances, yet the academe generally attempts to perpetuate this stereotype. The faculty post has become a clear profession with, as Cahn (1986) argued, both faculty saints and faculty scamps, and this profession, due to abuses and power struggles, has truly become a managed profession well within the public eye.

As shared governance attempts to succeed in such settings, there are clear issues of purpose, power, and performance. Contextualizing the issues helps dramatically, yet true progress will only be made when there is a clarification of expectations both from trustees and administrators and the faculty body. Sadly, it is the faculty body that finds the notion of shared governance most important, yet terribly unsupported, save for a few value-touching issues and concerns. Within this very context, the National Data Base on Faculty Involvement in Governance was designed to catalog and report what is happening with shared governance units, and perhaps suggest a future that is more productive and reflective of the need to ensure the academy as an environment for creative, intellectual thought that cares for the cognitive development of students and the growth of knowledge bases.

Chapter 2

Environments and Culture of Faculty Involvement in Governance

The climate and need for well-informed, well-intentioned decision-making in higher education has never been more important. The historical growth of colleges and universities resembles that of many other industries, with substantial specialization of certain segments, diversification of product lines, and branding of products. The exorbitant attention given to big-time collegiate athletics represents one form of "branding," as institutions work to develop very specific niche markets and to distribute their products at a competitive rate in any number of geographic areas. In particular, the rise in distributed education, whether formal degree-related or recreational, to foreign markets, the military, and specialty segments of the population demonstrate the growing diversification and definition of "higher learning."

The growth of higher education, however, has not been entirely corporate driven or negative. The proportion of adults with a college-level education is at an all-time high, universities are providing key research to fuel the economy, there is both a pre- and post-technology boom, and as never before, institutions are fiscally-savvy agencies with multiple revenue-streams and many leaders who have a strong business sense. This picture, however, does not resemble the institution of even 30 years ago. As college students wax and wane over majors and their intention on being "in college," spending time with activities and self-exploration, institutions focus on occupational pathways for students almost from their time of arrival (Selingo, 2000).

The climates of administrative behavior can be largely seen in the types of activities that contemporary college leaders must undertake (see for example, Twombly, 1988). The American Association of Community Colleges outlined a list of tasks (Shults, 2001) that include fiscal management, fund raising, human resource supervision, public relations, and time and stress management. These are hardly the images of previous decade's college presidents who were seen more as perhaps the best and brightest of the faculty who temporarily leave their love of teaching to assume a leadership position. The evolution of the presidency, much like that illustrated by Lucas (2000), probably includes a slow gradual shift of presidential responsibilities with increased levels of sophistication over time. Much like a glacier, though, changes in the position have been substantial, irreversible, and visible.

As the college president position at all types of institutions has changed, so to have supporting administrative positions. Increases in spending on administrative salaries have grown as one piece of evidence supporting the retooling of the management needed for contemporary colleges and universities. For example, presidential salary spending was up over 11% during the past three years, while faculty salary averages were up only 3.7% (Nicklin, 2001). The breadth of titles and areas of responsibility have also evolved substantially even within the past ten years. For example, in the area of institutional development, directors of major gifts have become directors of planned gifts or giving, directors of estate gifts, directors of major annual gifts, and so on. The same type of specialization has taken place through administrative ranks as individuals of specialized training manage and oversee facilities, grounds, investments, technology purchasing and support, etc.

But what about faculty members? Faculty roles have changed too, and reflect a very different professorate on campus than that which was in place 40 or 50 years ago. Faculty have a different level of sophistication that sprung up from the willingness to think differently by the faculty of the academic freedom movement of 30 years ago. The students and faculty who stormed campus administration buildings and revolted over *in loco parentis,* among other issues, have trained an entire generation of new faculty. And in many instances, the generation of faculty they trained, have now taught and mentored a second post 1970 generation of faculty. This second generation, which has assailed the college professorate within the last ten years (largely due, also, to the strong economy) have entered the workforce with different kinds of expectations and general thinking. Movement among positions in different institutions is common today, a practice that was seldom seen 20 years ago.

The perceived harsh and unpleasant quantification of research production has also become a major conversation among this generation of faculty. Questions about how many articles will 'get tenure' and what kind of teaching evaluation mean scores are necessary dominate new faculty orientations, mentoring programs, and professional associations, rather than questions about contributing to a knowledge base and working to help every student learn. This second generation has also entered the academy with a greater level of methodological sophistication, something that carries both positive and negative consequences. Publications and conversations certainly have a more intense level of reliability, but design ingenuity and content-driven research have decreased. Similarly, faculty are quickly categorized into "quantitative" and "qualitative" paradigms without regard for topical knowledge or content. In many departments, research design has begun to outweigh content expertise.

In many ways, this new generation of faculty members has taken the creativity and strength of independence of previous generations and attempted to institutionalize it. The impact has serious consequences, quite obviously for students, but in more subtle ways on individual campuses. New faculty are willing to get involved, but generally in areas that offer direct rewards. Service on research committees, human subjects, and technology committees are common for the new generation, while more traditional areas that involve the philosophical thinking, values, and actions of institutions are almost devoid of junior faculty. Institutions doubly suffer with few new faculty making lifelong commitments to institutions, instead moving on for better compensation packages, prestige, or taking advantage of perceived quality of life factors. This movement can be deflating to students in addition to providing an example that institutional loyalty is paycheck bound.

All but a few of this new generation are excitedly moving into areas of traditional academic administration, fueling the fire of administrative specialization to even greater extents. Instead of moving faculty into various assistant and associate dean roles, specialists in accreditation, human resource management, and fund raising are moving in. These faculty members generally get along with those of the generation who trained them, those appointed sparsely in the early 1980s and more abundantly in the late-1980s and early 1990s, but report conflicting experiences, attitudes, and disagreement with earlier generations of faculty.

And while newer faculty are beginning to more aggressively move into departmental chair positions, these administrative responsibilities become more appropriately seen as gateways to other academic-support administrative opportunities. Departmental chair experiences have begun to pave administrative paths into student affairs, institutional research, policy leadership, and even facilities and business management. Thus, the talent that once led the academic front of institutions has now been diffused into many different areas, and academic management has become much more of a niche career market and path. These tendencies have been even further reinforced by the increasing diversification of the college presidency, with many more presidents being appointed from non-academic affairs career paths and labor pools.

As this new generation of faculty members crafts their own unique legacy to higher education, they must find a generational-appropriate definition of what faculty involvement in governance can, should, and does mean. For many, involvement at the departmental level is substantial and politics involve senior faculty, department chairs, deans, and at times, a provost. Institution-wide involvement involves all of those plus other administrators, such as a dean of students, vice president for administration, the college president, and even board members. As the stakes become increasingly higher, faculty may find there is less they can do to make an immediate impact and that their voices make little difference in the daily lives of faculty.

Another consideration for new faculty is the inherent concern over tenure decisions and a desire not to upset or openly challenge those with tenure-granting power. The natural self-selection of those involved, then, presupposes a greater involvement in institutional matters by tenured faculty, and the dutiful work of departmental politics being undertaken by non-tenured faculty.

The political dimensions of faculty involvement can also be

overwhelming for new and senior faculty alike, as political positioning and lobbying by faculty, and sometimes staff can clearly illustrate the distribution of power within an institution. Law, medical, and engineering schools all maintain tremendous levels of political clout on virtually any campus, although medical and engineering schools tend to be the revenue producing, highly visible research centers that determine research university status. Indeed, engineering and medicine are the "showcase" colleges in many instances that highlight a university's rigor, with schools such as law and business occasionally making a mark on an institution's reputation. On many land-grant university campuses, agricultural studies are also dominant, particularly those active in federal and commercial research and development projects that consistently prove to be highly lucrative. The university or college-wide governance body brings these representatives together to claim equal debate and voice in institutional decision-making. These situations typically, though, serve as prompts for revenue producing colleges to showcase their concerns and dictate agendas for the university in an alternative setting. Individual faculty senators can make a tremendous difference, but generally, the golden rule applies: those with the gold make the rules.

Where does all of this leave faculty involvement in governance? Broadly, faculty members are pitted against a swelling administrative body and against each other to advance an agenda. In many situations, faculty are also pitted against students, who are often more organized, committed, and passionate about involvement and making a difference than their faculty counterparts. What agenda is undertaken, agreed to, and what actions are expected are often a source of debate heightened only by the ability of a faculty member, student, or administrator to meaningfully secure an institutional action that makes a meaningful difference in the lives of those on campus.

The other dimension that often proves crippling to the shared governance effort is a continual conversation and debate about what constitutes "governance." Although many see governance as an action that results in policy, behaviors, or specific actions, others want to see governance interpreted as institutional administration or management. The lack of resolution on this most basic question can debilitate an entire senate and result in greater levels of manipulation or neglect by administrators.

In community, technical, and junior colleges the situation may be substantially different. Much of the personnel attrition that four-year colleges and universities are dealing with now have been dealt with for the past decade. Despite a reported pending leadership crisis for community colleges (Katsinas & Kempner, 2001), the faculty employed by these institutions are stronger than ever before. Many have doctorates and can critically examine research and knowledge and databases, they find satisfaction with their environments, are stable, and many report purposively making the decision to be a community college teacher. Unlike previous generations who had secondary school teaching experience (Laabs, 1987), those in community college teaching ranks today have been especially trained for their work (Hawthorne, 1991), many even completing specialized community college teaching programs or certificates, such as those at Southern Illinois University or the University of Arkansas.

For these community college faculty, the political process is often more external in orientation. With a charge to be responsive to community needs and concerns, external bodies such as state-wide coordinating boards or advisory boards often recommend curricular changes with limited feedback from faculty. Also, many state legislators mandate to articulate two-year community college education and four-year bachelor degree program curricula have come at a tremendous cost: the cost of academic freedom to define syllabi, and at the expense of high-cost, high-need vocational and occupational programs. Many colleges find it attractive to offer transfer-oriented programs that can serve large numbers of students rather than programs such as welding, which is expensive to operate and requires a low student-faculty ratio. All done regardless of need, these articulation agreements have the potential to divide faculty and place them politically in opposition to each other. Yet, these statewide articulation programs do open a pathway to bachelor's degree attainment that has not been open in the past for many students, and makes for a more efficient transfer process. In a sense, these agreements are the product, and evidence of, a systems approach to publicly supported higher education.

Administrative Trust

The basic notion of political behavior is that there is a competition for resources. As Wildavsky (1988) and Bowen (1980) argued, public bodies continually grow and consume greater resources, and these resources are in constant demand and are continually consumed. This consumption leads to more activity and more perceived need, and while more is being done, administrative attention, particularly of late, is toward quality and efficiency. For faculty members this can be particularly problematic and can cause an even greater resentment and lack of trust of administrators.

The resentment and lack of trust can be based on surging administrative expenditures in comparison to shrinking faculty resources. As administrators create and fund new initiatives, faculty can find fewer and fewer resources to attend meetings or conferences, purchase journals and books, and fund research. To a large extent, as an increasingly mobile administrative workforce moves from institution to institution, the more-resident faculty find difficulty, and ultimately lack of trust, for administrators who seem to have an "arrive and devour" approach to academic management.

Embedded in part of this conversation about trust is the idea of administrative versus faculty movement. For many administrators, there is an unwritten move-out (to another institution) to move-up (career advancement; title upgrade) attitude to career management, and the typical life-span of an administrative position is around seven years. Ironically, it is during the seventh and typically first-tenured year, that faculty members begin to realize a freedom and comfort that allows them an access to campus life and decision-making open only to those secure in their employment. The result of the timing and length of careers and tenure coincide in such a way that when administrators arrive in a position or on a campus and immediately begin taking action, only a segment of the faculty body is in a position to respond from a vantage point of security and institutional history. Perhaps, then, this continual responsiveness rather than assertiveness creates a feeling of distrust or resentment by faculty to the growing administrative ranks.

These ideas about trust and respect must be considered in the context of the changing nature of the administrator. As college administrators are called upon to do more and different things, their compensation changes. For a dean of students who is expected to be on campus four or five evenings a week in addition to regular office-hours, the institution must be prepared to pay a competitive wage. Similarly, those working throughout student affairs, fund raising, public affairs, risk management, alumni and government relations, etc., expect to be paid competitive wages determined by a professional market. This is also true for academic administrators who not only have a great volume of work, but interpersonal driven work that requires sound judgment in addition to content-specific knowledge particularly as related to agency law (Miles, 1997A). The risks involved are also greater; the risks of lawsuits, complaints and grievances in bargaining units, disgruntled employees, and so on, all mean that institutions have to be better prepared to compensate frontline administrators consistent with market practices. And while many institutions utilize a peer-group rating as a mechanism for determining faculty pay, they similarly use peer-groups based on responsibilities for determining administrative pay. The difference tends to be largely that administrative tasks and compensations increase at a faster rate due to similarities with private-sector markets that have greater flexibility and often greater resources to compensate professionals.

In addition to salary, benefits paid to these positions can create hostility on the part of faculty. While administrators may get substantial travel budgets to stay abreast of legal decisions, risk management issues, or the latest in fund raising, many faculty members have limited or nonexistent travel budgets. For some Division I athletic institutions, for example, a tour of similar stadiums or athletic venues around the country can have a substantial impact on event coordination and planning, and sending a team of athletic administrators to visit the venues around the country for a week might not require a second thought. Yet, presenting a research-based paper at a regional conference may get virtually no financial support. Administrators will argue that travel with direct economic benefit outweighs faculty attendance at meetings. At many institutions, travel is only supported if a faculty member is on a program of speakers, and some institutions even regulate which conferences or meetings warrant funding. And by indicating which conferences and meetings warrant funding, administrators and perhaps a select group of powerful faculty can regulate which kinds of scholarship, topics, and even research methodologies can and will be valued.

Computer upgrades, office furniture, long-distance telephone access, franking privileges, and even business cards, letterhead, parking spaces, and party and reception invitations can combine to create a society of perceived haves (administrators) and have-nots (faculty). At some institutions, administrators can have airline tickets prepaid by the university, a service denied to faculty who must seek reimbursements. These are the 'little things' that comprise a culture, a community, and an environment. And it is this culture that develops as much of an impact on faculty decisions for involvement as other processural issues about consultation and the value of dialogue and participation.

The idea of valuing dialogue has linkages to the process of how faculty and staff are involved in governance. As illustrated in the previous chapter, faculty governance units can be used for different kinds of reactions and actions, ranging from consultation to sharing power. When there is ambiguity about what the expected roles are to be, trust among faculty and administrators can be substantially threatened.

The threat comes predominantly in the form of what administrators are willing to put on a shared governance agenda, including academic as well as academic-support areas. Restructuring a division of student affairs, for example, can have a substantial impact on how faculty work with students, how faculty-student grievances are resolved, etc., yet this type of activity is generally not presented to faculty governance units, even as a matter of information. Fund raising campaigns, computer/mainframe system upgrades, student life issues, and business operations and facilities procedures all greatly impact the campus environment and life, and failing to consult, inform, and collaborate with faculty can easily yield a culture that at least has the appearance of not communicating and giving way to open distrust.

To cast the population of administrators into any clear generalization is problematic, and it should be noted that many administrative offices do in fact work to incorporate faculty views and insights into decision-making. Divisions of student affairs are perhaps the most receptive to initiating faculty involvement. These divisions incorporate a host of decision-making committees and task forces, utilize faculty groups to analyze data, and to make policy recommendations. In other administrative areas, such as grounds maintenance or tele-commuting, faculty may rarely be involved in conversations about planning for campus. This selectivity of involvement in many cases can ultimately lead to questions of responsive campus citizenship and trust.

Faculty Trust

Do faculty trust administrators? Do faculty trust each other? Do administrators trust faculty or other administrators? The college campus has most certainly changed, and the broad array of administrative career paths and faculty teaching domains similarly provide clear indications that hyper-specialization has become common on campus. As institutions attempt to "grow," the need for administrative posts has increased dramatically. Since 1993, the number of full-time faculty on campus has grown from 545,706 to 568,719 in 1997, a four percent growth, while the number of full-time administrators running campuses has grown from 493,388 to 536,115, or nearly a nine percent growth during the same period of time (Chronicle of Higher Education Almanac, 1995; 2001).

The growth of administrative positions reflects the increased complexity of contemporary college management. Institutions are more engaged in major gift and planned fund raising, event and conference management, and globalization. As key university services are outsourced, professionals are needed to supervise contracts and maintain profit margins, activities that were present but less visible in previous decades.

The faculty response to the growth of administrative positions has been to feel less empowered on campus and to trust administrators less. Although this level of distrust might be unfounded, there is a feeling among faculty that "they," that is, administrators, are growing much faster than faculty numbers and resources, and that administrators do so at the expense of the "real" purpose of the institution, that is teaching and research. Some of this may be accurate and some may be terribly inaccurate. In the competition for resources and students, institutions must become more savvy and employ staff to manage the institution's image and to seek out resources that were once plentiful from state or other funds. At the same time, the national reliance on part-time and temporary faculty has become extreme, and in key course sequences, namely general education, these part-time faculty are the norm. The feelings of distrust, then, become quite natural as administrative positions increase and the number of full-time tenure, tenure-track faculty decrease or increase only moderately.

Yet another area of growth in distrust of administrators by faculty has concerns the details of institutional life. While administrators obtain generous travel funds, staff assistance, and well appointed offices, faculty resources remain the same. From the faculty perspective, how is a national reputation maintained with travel support that is virtually nonexistent? An administrative reply is to seek external funding through grants and contracts, essentially penalizing the faculty member with more work to obtain the resources necessary simply to succeed in the job the person was hired to do. With a multitude of new administrative posts being added, it is easy to see how faculty members can interpret an administrative bloating at their expense.

Distrust works in both ways, however, as administrators can easily look at the professorate with a combination of envy and disrespect. Although few argue about the high intelligence levels of faculty members, the autonomy of work can lead an administrator locked into strict office hours to believe that faculty do not work hard enough. Coupled with substantial questions about the sabbatical as a form of faculty development and widespread rumors about various individual faculty members teaching performance (or lack of), administrators can see long hours unrecognized or unappreciated. This may be particularly true on campus, where the primary focus of the institutional mission continues to be faculty teaching students. This distrust can then be further heightened by the performance of faculty governance units where the majority of members do not attend meetings, senates fail to tackle the difficult issues of campus, and these bodies trivialize what administrators believe to be important, dominant issues on campus.

Despite the apparent distrust, there generally are strong levels of co-existence and mutual respect for certain administrative posts. The model of academic administrator preparation being that of a faculty member growing in a position through service as a chair and dean can indeed lead to high levels of trust and respect. The trend of other administrators moving into the presidency or the career college president, however, run the potential of greatly increasing levels of distrust and disrespect.

These issues of trust and respect are not universal, however, as many regional universities and community colleges find that individual relationships developed over long periods of time can greatly enhance institutional performance. At many community colleges, for example, senior academic administrators are seen less as an extension of the faculty working in their behalf to administrators performing the key managerial functions of college life. Similarly, at many liberal arts institutions senior academic affairs professionals are seen simply as those on loan to serve a higher purpose. In these types of situations, administrators are viewed with extremely high levels of respect and trust. This reputation, however, can be greatly damaged or enhanced through the treatment of governance bodies.

Part-Time Faculty

The use and reliance of colleges and universities on part-time faculty has increased dramatically over the past 20 years. The occasional adjunct was once used to cover a clinical section or offer an applied seminar, but has now become a common approach to covering introduction and large-lecture courses. Part-time faculty have become a frequently used source of inexpensive labor that carries little long-term obligation and oversight. As Karabell (1998) noted, part-time faculty quality can be difficult to assess and schedule. For the causal student this can be a particularly challenging notion, not knowing who a faculty member is or whether the teaching style is compatible and can lead to a gambling feeling among students.

The case for part-time faculty use can be compelling. These faculty members typically have a love for students and teaching, and undertake the activity for the satisfaction of the experience rather than the salary. Part-time faculty members are also often referred to as "clinical faculty" because they have current, up to date skills that reflect current practice and the latest of the current work force's advances. In many vocational programs, part-time faculty are even favored as the combination of their current skills and exposure to the business world work to the advantage of students. This type of relationship can also help the institution become better rooted in the community, as ties with business and industry are strengthened. Additionally, with primary incomes other than teaching, many part-time faculty are willing to teach for little money and few benefits, allowing institutions to capitalize on their expertise. From a managerial perspective, part-time faculty also allow an institution a greater flexibility of scheduling courses, offering only what sections are required by enrollment.

Conversely, part-time faculty members have a history of being taken advantage of in terms of pay and benefits, and at many institutions the student-to-part-time faculty member ratio is significantly higher than that for full-time, tenure-track faculty. And at some colleges and universities, part-time employment opportunities are patched together from different institutions to make a full-time job. For these faculty, the lower pay for a heightened work load is a major issue and an exploitation of labor. And from an institutional perspective, using part-time faculty members on a semester-to-semester basis can create an inconsistency of instructors, courses offered, teaching and advising quality, and can create problems for students as they try to register for courses in a sequence leading to a timely graduation.

The boundary of benefit and abuse can be difficult to determine, and has something to do with internationality. If institutions truly see the use of part-time faculty as a benefit to student learning, then the environment for faculty to be involved in policy formation is more pronounced. Similarly, institutions that either overtly or covertly exploit part-time faculty are less likely to involve faculty in governance. Institutions with bargaining units have typically performed better at protecting the rights of part-time faculty and have gone so far as to construct formal salary schedules for part-timers with various experience and degree levels. Yet, there remains an almost universal attitude of disrespect for part-timers. Karabel (1998) noted "(a)nd capable or not, adjuncts have little reason to be loyal to the institution that pays them. They are given no benefits, no respect, no office and little money. They rarely interact with other faculty, and when they do, they are treated much like temp workers at a corporate office." (p. 200)

Use of part-time faculty members has grown from 369,768 in 1993 to 421,094 in only five years (Chronicle of Higher Education Almanac, 1995; 2001). These faculty members earn as much as 30% less than their full-time tenure-track colleagues in the California Community College System, even though they comprise over 40% of that system's instructional faculty (California State Auditor, 2001). The statistics in other states and other systems are equally disparate, and without certain academic freedom protections, they are more likely to be at risk of contract non-renewal due to collegiality or academic thinking or criticism.

A tangential concern about the rise of part-time faculty may be the desirability of an academic career. As Rojstaczer (1999) noted, the academic life has changed greatly during the past four or five decades, has become much more political, and is less respected in the community and the public. As colleges and universities cling to old-economy models of management, there are entire cadres of potential faculty who find the prospects for greater salaries, greater teamwork, and greater creativity in the private sector.

Despite the reliance on part-time faculty, institutions have not developed these employee pools as a pipeline to the tenure-track. In fact, serving as a part-time faculty member may actually do more harm to the tenure-track applicant, casting the would-be faculty member in the light of someone who could not get on the tenure-track to start, and probably should not after temping. Additionally, the teaching-heavy workload of a temporary faculty member works against having the time to conduct research and publish, both greatly valued commodities at virtually every level of institution (Karabel, 1998).

Even though part-time faculty make up such a substantial portion of the faculty population, few caveats exist to include them in institutional governance. Some institutions will allow part-time faculty a vote in proportionality to their teaching load, for example, and others will allow the temporary faculty member to serve on an institutional committee or even on a faculty senate. Stipulations for this service, though, are often many and relate to time base, institutional history, and academic degree. Thus, even faculty members who have the power to define policy related to their own governments have not embraced their part-time colleagues as equals. The result, in addition to there being little incentive to be a part-time faculty member, is the continuation of an academic caste system, self-ruled, that places the titles and rewards of the tenure system as dominant in faculty life. As an example to their students, faculty seem to be symbolically saying "do not recognize part time students for we do not recognize part-time faculty." Ironically, the voices of many faculty members and administrators report the exact opposite, stating that the campus should embrace and welcome part-time, non-traditional students, suggesting something even more of a "do-as-I-say-not-as-I-do" mentality among campus citizens.

The tradition of attitudes toward part-time faculty even becomes self-fulfilling, as those who do make it onto the tenure track enjoy the privileges without championing their former colleagues. And this very class system, one in which faculty do have control, becomes a major barrier to achieving academic democracy. Therefore, if institutions truly value citizen voices, there is an underlying need to define a policy that allows participants entry into the decision-making process, and this then opens a sub-textual conversation about representation within representation. If governance units are indeed designed to represent the will of the people, they must make an authentic effort to truly represent these constituents and their concerns. Representation need not be based entirely on the notion of direct-representation, e.g., only part-time faculty representing part-time faculty, but there must be a consensual understanding and commitment to represent the issues and needs of others. And this is part of the very problematic implementation of any representative democracy, as those needs and concerns represented are often power-based and influenced by those with resources.

Student Participation in Governance

The involvement of students in institutional governance is a relatively sporadic, yet permanent component of higher education, which ranges from little to no involvement on some campuses to full voting student membership on a board of trustees (Miles, 1997B). Students have generally staked a claim on some self-governance domains, typically oversight for their own organizations through both student organization officers and an over-arching policy function through an association of all enrolled students, such as student government association, although in many instances students feel that they do not have the power to influence the systems and structures of colleges and universities (Williamson, 1984). These student governments typically have powers to regulate student organization behaviors within the limits of a constitution that has administrative consent, and they have the authority to impose and allocate student fee revenue.

Student government associations take on a variety of forms, including representative bodies where representation is based on where students live, on academic major, on enrollment status, coalitions of student organizations, and even resemble town halls that include all students. The challenges they face, however, are quite similar to those faced by faculty governance bodies including full participation, member commitment, role clarity, and equity.

Student activism has been a major part of higher education since the founding of Harvard College in the 1600s, although this activism received little attention until the 1940s when non-traditional students who had returned from military service in World War II placed substantial demands on the existing higher education system (Cartwright, 1995). Students suddenly needed different types of services, such as those to accommodate a spouse and child, different types of financial aid assistance, course schedules that better facilitated full-time employment, and even the offering of classes in the evening. In the public eye, however, the student activism of the late 1960s and early 1970s was considerably more powerful and had a substantial impact on faculty, administrators, and policy makers.

Part of the primary concern for student participation in governance was quite simply that the lack of involvement resulted in widespread protest and activism, and the lack of institutional response drove the situation even further to breed national organizations to use student activism as a means of political agenda setting (Michener, 1971). By institutional leaders and traditions failing to recognize the radically different needs of students during this era, they continued to try and force a template of behavior and expectation on students who had very different notions about life expectations. These ranged from freedom of association and speech to self-presentation and religious experimentation. The ultimate institutional response was a substantial change in how students are viewed, the changing of major policies such as the death of *in loco parentis,* and the granting of power to students in certain areas.

Altbach and Cohen (1989) have noted major differences in activism in college student attitudes during the past 20 years. Students currently on campus have been called apathetic and conservative, but Altbach and Cohen have noted that there is indeed a great deal of activism, on a much smaller scale and contained within certain parameters. They noted the lack of a major national issue as something that has prevented student activism from spreading from campus to campus, and instead, pockets of student power have been demonstrated on selected campuses. Broadly, though, many of these student groups have not been seen as involved as in previous decades, although they have been given the label of having the "fashion" without the "passion" (Miller & Nelson, 1996).

Student activism has seemingly changed from reactionary politics based on national issues to more planned action steps toward change. For example, there are still protests and demonstrations related to issues such as the anti-apartheid movement on college campuses in the 1980s, but current activism has focused more on raising awareness (the Take Back the Night movement and demonstrations) and involvement in community service.

The current role of the student in governance is strongly linked to the notion of community governance, also known as campus governance. The community governance frame of thinking calls on students, staff, administrators, and faculty to join together to make critical decisions and respond to important issues dealing with the welfare of the institution and institutional life (Botzek,

1972; Miles, 1997B). Schlesinger and Baldridge (1982), though, have noted that despite institutional intentions, students are generally reported to have less authority in decision making, and when placed on governing boards, for example, tend to be excluded from voting privileges.

Arising from the discussion of who should be involved in what types of decision-making and who has "rights" in the areas of campus life, student governance structures tend to have clearly defined realms of responsibility. These responsibilities typically relate to student self-governance, including the disbursement of student generated fee monies, the allocation of privileges and campus resources, and even disciplinary proceedings. Student self-governance, however, is not typically confined to their activities related to curriculum and institutional quality of life factors and decisions. Student governance bodies, therefore, regularly confront campus issues, speaking out on various topics ranging from outsourcing contracts to state higher education appropriations. In almost nearly every scenario, however, these actions are not spelled out in constitutions or founding charters to allow for an enforcing power to be present behind decisions, meaning student governance bodies can recommend measures, but the campus and campus leaders have no obligation to accept, respond to, or acknowledge the measure. Campus leaders are in positions to formally recognize actions taken by student government bodies, and often accept or at least formally respond to their actions for the purpose of building community and a positive environment on campus.

Regardless of institutional response, students tend to receive a great deal from involvement in campus life, ranging from enhanced social interaction and persistence to greater satisfaction with the college experience (Albrecht, Carpenter, & Sivo, 1994; Boyer, 1987; Williams & Winston, 1985). In addition to stronger positive feelings about the institution and enhanced student success, involvement also forms as a substantial mechanism for teaching students about issues that organizations and institutions face, and the complexity of decision-making and problem solving in real world environments (Goldberg, 1980).

The types of student organizations that provide opportunities for involvement are multiple, numbering in the hundreds on many college campuses. These include fraternities, sororities, special interest groups, service organizations, etc., and almost all campuses make use of an over-arching student government association. This association provides generally the broadest mechanism for working with a student body and, in most cases, provides the most powerful tool for making decisions within student populations. Little to no research currently exists on the parallel behaviors and structures between faculty governance associations and student governance associations, although there is at least anecdotal evidence that the two tend to be seen in radically different lights. For example, at The University of Alabama, one of the strongest student government associations on a college campus was composed of diversity in excess to campus proportions and in excess of the faculty senate, yet the senate provided public statements about the need for further integration and greater diversity. In a constitutional convention at that campus, over 25% of the student population voted for a constitution, yet the existing faculty senate typically struggled with getting a quorum to attend a meeting (see Miller, 1998).

The Alabama case study provides the clearest example of why student involvement in governance is important to the conversation about faculty involvement in governance. There is the obvious dimension of the need for an institutional culture that respects democracy and needs to reflect this value in both student and faculty camps. Institutions in their language and behavior, though, seem to have expectations and actually encourage student participation in campus life, yet little encouragement is provided to participation in faculty governance outside of home academic departments. Further, the expectation of faculty for responsible student life is difficult to defend when the faculty expectation seems lower and in fact less organized than student government. Yet, the institution seems to somehow value faculty input more than student or staff input, and there must be an emergence of dialogue about how these forms of democracy can co-exist and how they can work together to better frame a culture and life on campus that cultivates the individual. Similarly, the research on student involvement needs to be turned to questions of faculty involvement, particularly on the topics of work place satisfaction and leading the democratic life that respects diversity of thinking and living.

Impact on Faculty Involvement in Governance

The purpose of faculty governance is to enhance institutional decision-making, and the environment and culture of both the processes and the mechanisms of decision-making are vital. As alluded to in this chapter, there are many institutionally specific variables that can impact the performance and results of faculty governance actions. Campbell (2000) has suggested that personnel and personalities have a great deal to do with both, stressing the power of individual interpretations of responsibilities as major sources of difficulty. Rosovsky (1990) similarly noted the power of individualism to either make the shared governance process work or stagnate.

There are over-arching themes, though, that arise from a combination of literature, research, and personal narratives that suggest a similarity between many institutions. The notion of trust, for example and addressed here, has a great deal to do with whether a faculty senate or council can make a meaningful decision that is accepted across campus, or whether administrators can trust faculty to take large, institutional considerations into account in making choices and decisions. Other issues that have a potential to impact the culture of decision-making include budget practices, enrollment revenue reliance, research intensity, bargaining unit status, reliance on part-time faculty, faculty retention issues, and faculty and administrative belief sets.

Budget practices and revenue reliance can force an institution to either conceal or expose the institution's fiscal health. When budgeting in exclusionary, for instance, feelings of distrust may rise and questions of funding priorities are either repressed or brought to light. A subset of that conversation is to what extent an institution is reliant on student generated revenues, correlating the importance of caring for faculty needs with enrollment. Similarly, in research intense environments there may be little attention given to shared governance by faculty regardless of administrative enthusiasm. So these two dimensions of teaching and research suggest a need for a reward structure for participation be present. Even in community and junior colleges, a lack of formal rewards for service activities have been noted (Seagren, Wheeler, Creswell,

Miller, & VanHorn-Grassmeyer, 1994). And on this issue are some of the strengths of bargaining units in defining and defending faculty workloads issues and structuring contracts that respect an active academic citizenry. Yet, almost *de facto*, the use of bargaining units, while building avenues for faculty participation, at the same time potentially malign administrative trust, although this is not always the case.

One area that bargaining units have spent an increasing number of resources and time on is part-time faculty. Aronowitz (2000), among many others, has argued that the exploitation of part-time faculty members is one of the most disgraceful practices in academe, and indeed, an institution with a heavy reliance on part-time faculty will have a much different culture than one with a resident faculty. In an environment with a large part-time faculty base, curricular decisions are often removed from faculty units and made through administrative offices, part-time faculty are excluded from budgetary decisions, and part-time faculty sometimes lack an even basic loyalty to the institution and therefore are not well positioned to make important decisions. Also, part-time faculty members are often used on such a temporary basis that administrative bodies by default ignore them. The resulting caste system that is forged among faculty both externally and internally creates notions of disparity and mistrust among faculty themselves as well as among faculty and administrators.

The idea of length of faculty service also impacts full-time, tenure/tenure-track faculty. In institutional settings where there is high faculty attrition, the tasks of governance become the responsibility of the senior faculty; often those with lengthy institutional memory and a strong sense of self-governance tradition. These situations have the potential to keep junior faculty excluded from the governance process or create such an "insiders-club" that junior faculty choose not to be involved. The opposite is also true, where large numbers of new faculty take over bodies and expel the knowledge and traditions safeguarded among the senior ranks. To the administrator, this may all look impractical and inefficient, furthering the ideas of disrespect or involvement merely for faculty placation.

Perhaps most important to the faculty involvement in governance cause are the belief sets that faculty and administrators bring to their positions about life in democratic organizations. Management literature typically defends the democratic workplace (Evans, 1999), but if the administrator does not value a diversity of opinions and ideas, then faculty governance has a strong likelihood of failure. If faculty arrive on campus with no expectation or interest in involvement, the shared governance process can also be killed from the inside. Indeed, the creation of the entrepreneur faculty member committed to research or specialized sub-disciplines does little to advance the notion of academic community. If faculty members do not believe they should value and expect an academic democracy, then quite simply, they will not have it.

A key function for faculty and administrators to consider is the role, form, and practice of academic democracy, and whether this democracy has a place on campus. Will the corporate university have a place for dissenting points of view on institutional matters? And if faculty expect to have a role in campus matters, what kind of role models are their governance bodies for students on their campus? What kind of responsible citizenship do faculty members need to undertake to be effective advocates for democracy? And what kind of knowledge and education need to be provided to faculty and administrators to grow a healthy shared decision-making process? Indeed, faculty involvement in governance has benefits and problems depending upon point of view and issue of consideration, but at-risk is the more fundamental question of whether faculty will have the possibility of involvement.

Administrators who have risen through academic ranks can have powerful, positive impacts on the future of faculty involvement in governance, and have a responsibility to champion this value to non-academic managers who seem to be permeating the campus community. Similarly, those currently involved have an obligation to act responsibly, and seek out the political middle-ground that is so important to the art of compromise and the future of college communities.

Chapter 3

The National Data Base on Faculty Involvement in Governance Project

Research projects and national initiatives are driven by any number of sources, both those of national emergency and those of personal interest. The National Data Base on Faculty Involvement in Governance was founded on a combination of these extremes, and is based largely on a collegial inter-play among emerging scholars around the United States. The primary motivation was a combination of both personal interest and survival through tenure and promotion activities, the recognition that faculty members have a role in shared governance, and that ignoring this responsibility places academic decision-making in unusual and at times compromised situations.

So the motivating questions of "do faculty legitimately have a role in shared governance activities?" "What kinds of roles are to be undertaken, and who provides the leadership necessary to make a difference in how colleges operate?" framed the work of the Data Base. To give guidance and structure to the examination, a board of directors was established and data were collected, forming more of a cooperative research project than a traditional data base. The result, however, was largely the same as formative advances were made in understanding who and how collaborative academic decision-making is and has been made.

From a personal perspective, participating faculty often had a common denominator: a quest for an active research agenda that could lead to research and publication. For tenure purposes this was a functional motivation, but for personal purposes, the desire to share informative, constructive research had a much more philosophical and constructive dimension. All participating faculty and staff were committed to viewing a role of faculty in shared governance, and the work of the collaborative gave form to that work.

The resulting publications and reports were helpful reminders that the work of the ivory tower not always be isolated and theoretical, and that good research by concerned faculty can have a meaningful impact on how universities live.

Founding the Data Base

The basis of this book is the National Data Base on Faculty Involvement in Governance (NDBFIG) project that was run at The University of Alabama between 1994 and 1999, and completed at San Jose State University in 2000 and 2001. The project received support from the Vice President for Academic Affairs at Alabama, and the College of Education at San Jose State University.

The roots of the NDBFIG project were established in a research project developed at the University of Nebraska-Lincoln's (UNL) Center for the Study of Higher and Postsecondary Education. The recently-established Center conducted a host of research projects in an effort to better establish its place within the academic community and particularly within the home department of the Center, the Department of Educational Administration in the UNL Teachers College. The project was originally conceptualized as an extension of much of the department chair research conducted by research fellows associated with the Center. The survey was conducted under the auspices of Professor Alan Seagren, with labor provided by Dan Wheeler and Michael Miller, with Wheeler providing content direction and Miller coordinating the research design. In that vein, the research was intended to be a component of academic leadership, how decisions are made on campus, and further, how decision-making can be improved to respond to various needs, activities, and constituent responses.

The initial investigation was comprised of a three-round Delphi study of faculty senate presidents about barriers to faculty involvement in governance. The major finding of this work was the importance of mutual trust and respect between administrators and faculty in decision-making. The work was published in 1993, and no further work was completed on the project, as the Center research fellows focused on their collaborative research with the National Community College Chair Academy.

Faculty and students at The University of Alabama identified the research findings in late 1993 and early 1994 through their own research on the topic of faculty involvement in governance. Dr. David Masoner, then Chair of the Higher Education Program at Alabama and later Provost at William Jennings Bryan College in Tennessee, collaborated with the doctoral student Thomas McCormack to adapt the survey for use in statewide data collection. This adaptation was the initial establishment of the NDBFIG, with a researcher from Nebraska joining the Alabama team to conduct the research. The adapted survey was conducted among state colleges and universities in Alabama, and provided the data for McCormack's doctoral dissertation (see McCormack, 1995). This dissertation data provided the field pilot test of the NDBFIG survey instrument. Minor adjustments were made to the survey, and under the guidance of the three researchers at Alabama, the NDBFIG was formalized.

Using a network of research associates who had ties with the Nebraska Center, the updated survey instrument was distributed at over 30 colleges and universities around the United States between 1995 and 1999. All data were housed in the Higher Education Administration Program at the University of Alabama, with analysis support provided by the Bureau of Educational Research headed by Dr. Harold Bishop and legal counsel provided by Professor Albert Miles.

The governing board of the NDBFIG project was established in 1996 after initial data sets were developed and publication of research findings were underway. The board provided general direction for the research initiative, including the development of various phases. Members of the board of directors of the NDBFIG are shown in Figure 2. The board met at various times, and was chaired by Dr. Richard Newman then at the University of Arkansas, at Monticello, and Dr. Carl Boening from Shelton State Community College in Tuscaloosa, Alabama. The board ceased operation in the 1999-2000 academic year once the final data collection efforts had begun. Dr. Myron Pope followed Dr. Michael Miller as the coordinator of the project from the University of Alabama campus. A listing of scholars affiliated with the NDBFIG project, both in terms of collaborating on various dimensions of the research and assisting in data collection, are shown in Figure 3.

Figure 2
Members of the NDBFIG Board of Directors

Board Member	*Institutional Affiliation at Time of Service*
Lindsay Barker	University of New South Wales
Camilla Benton	Bevill State Community College
Thomas A. Bila	Western New England College
Carl H. Boening	Shelton State Community College
Dann Husmann	University of Wisconsin
Glenn Nelson	University of Pittsburgh
Richard E. Newman	University of Arkansas-Monticello
Jennifer Evans Payne	University of Alabama
Myron Pope	Alabama Southern Community College
Alan T. Seagren	University of Nebraska
Thomas Ware, Jr.	Bevill State Community College

The notion of a collaborative research project not bound by a single institution was driven in part by the ability of faculty and staff members at different institutions to engage in a shared research project. The result was numerous perspectives and ideas about how to approach various dimensions of the research project, and each of the affiliated scholars brought different visions of individuals projects to the NDBFIG. Largely, affiliated scholars took part in activities by collaborating on writing, revising and/or distributing survey instruments, data entry and analysis, and presentation of research findings. In some instances, affiliated scholars were appointed on a part-time basis to the faculty of the Higher Education Administration Program at the University of Alabama, to teach a class. Such was the case for Dr. Richard Newman, for example, who was appointed as a clinical faculty member in the Higher Education Administration Program to teach a specialized course on college athletics and the involvement of faculty athletic representatives and faculty co-governance activities in managing intercollegiate athletic programs.

Qualifications for affiliated scholars varied from graduate students working on advanced degrees to established faculty and administrators at different types of institutions. Dr. Camilla Benton from Bevill State Community College in Alabama, for example, was a provost; Dr. L. Rayburn Brooks was a college president. Brian Carlisle and Jane Glazebrook Bartee, however, were graduate students studying higher education. The primary benefit to these diverse titles, areas of responsibility, and institutional typology, was to gain as many different perspectives on faculty governance as possible, and to give the research project a greater depth that would have otherwise been possible if only scholars or faculty senators were involved.

Figure 3
Scholars Affiliated with the NDBFIG Project

Scholar	Year	Institutional Affiliation
Lara A. Anderson	1996-1998	Universities of Nebraska/Alabama
Kang Bai	1996-1998	Troy State University Dothan
L. Rayburn Brooks	1997-1998	Northwest Technical Institute
Jane Glazebrook Bartee	1999-2000	University of Wyoming
Camilla Benton	1996-1998	Bevill State Community College
Charles Brown	1997-1998	University of Alabama
Brian A. Carlisle	1997-1998	University of Alabama
Niel A. Edmunds	1994-1995	University of Nebraska
Brian J. Garavalia	1996-1997	Valdosta State University
J. Francisco Hidalgo	1999-2000	San Jose State University
James Hood	1997-1998	Madison Area Technical College
James F. Maddox	1995-1996	Friends University
Thomas McCormack	1994-1999	Marion Military Institute
Jennifer Miles	1996-1997	University of Alabama
Gary Miller	1996-1997	Biola University
Richard E. Newman	1995-1997	University of Arkansas-Monticello
Myron Pope	1998-2001	Universities of Alabama/Oklahoma
Margaret Rice	1999-2000	University of Alabama
Alan T. Seagren	1995-1996	University of Nebraska
Steve Vacik	1995-1998	Bevill State Community College

Phases of Data Base Work

Data collection followed very specific guidelines and priorities as determined by the appointed board of directors. Individual projects were aligned in thematic categories early in 1995, to allow for resource planning. The project received support from the College of Education at the University of Alabama, as well as several private donors. The basic strategy adopted by the board was to profile what was going on, broadly, with faculty governance units, to look at those who provide leadership to faculty governance, to provide some sense of who impacts shared governance, to identify trends and issues, and to look internally at a couple of faculty governance bodies.

In 1995, samples of 100 faculty members were selected at six institutions, including three research universities, two comprehensive universities, and one liberal arts college. The baseline data collection instrument was utilized and was distributed on each campus. The sample was selected randomly at each institution. During 1996, ten institutions (five comprehensive universities and five research universities) were surveyed with the same instrument, again drawing on random samples of 100 faculty members at each institution. In the 1997 academic year, five liberal arts colleges and ten community colleges were surveyed with a revised instrument (cells of 100 faculty each), and in 1998 three additional research universities were surveyed, again including random samples of 100 faculty at each institution. In the fall of 1998, 350 faculty governance unit participants were surveyed, in 1999, 400 governance unit leaders were surveyed, and in 2000, 400 community college faculty governance unit leaders were surveyed. Additionally, in 1999, a special survey of motivation was distributed to 100 faculty governance unit leaders, and in 2001, an additional survey of 300 faculty governance unit leaders was undertaken to address special issues, such as skills and stressors of leadership. Between 1998 and 2000, a number of internal decision-making observations were conducted, as were three projects designed to look at the trends and issues in faculty governance. Results of these surveys are presented in the following chapters, along with a more detailed description of sampling procedures.

Phase I: Faculty Profiles

The initial phase of the NDBFIG project was the description of how faculty see their roles in governance and generally address the issue of what role faculty see themselves as having. Specifically, the project addressed the questions of:

• What do faculty see as their dominant roles in the governance process?

• How do faculty perceive their involvement in governance, both in procedural and substantitive domains?

• What does an ideal shared governance environment include?

This segment of the project was initiated with a three-round Delphi survey in 1990, and was adapted and initially used with faculty at the University of Alabama at Birmingham and Tuscaloosa, and at Auburn University in Alabama. Data collection continued during the next six years at various institutions based on personal contacts, and surveys were typically distribute to faculty through inter-campus mail procedures. Members of the board of directors typically volunteered to distributed the survey on their campuses, and scholars affiliated with the project also distributed the survey on their campuses. Additionally, by distributing the survey on different campuses, comparative statistics were offered to develop institutional reports, and these reports were distributed to a combination of faculty governance leaders and academic administrators.

A total of 34 colleges and universities participated in this segment of data collection. As representative samples, some of the institutions that provided data for this phase of the NDBFIG project are listed in Figure 4.

Figure 4.
Sample Institutions Participating in NDBFIG Phase 1

Institution Participating	Year
Alabama Southern Community College	1997
Auburn University	1994
Bevill State Community College	1996
Biola University	1995
Friends University	1995
Los Angeles Chiropractic College	1996
Madison Area Technical College	1998
Marion Military Academy	1996
Northwestern State University	1996
Northwest Technical Institute	1996
San Jose State University	1999
Stillman College	1997
Texas College	1996
University of Alabama	1994
University of Alabama at Birmingham	1995
University of Arkansas at Monticello	1996
University of Nebraska	1995
University of Mary	1995
University of Wisconsin	1996
Valdosta State University	1997
Western New England College	1996

Phase II: Faculty Governance Leaders

The second phase of the NDBFIG project focused on the individuals who organize and lead faculty governance units. The board specifically identified the need to better understand this population of leadership in order to make valid recommendations on the procedures of shared governance. Central to this are questions that might suggest how these faculty leaders make decisions and their views on the idea of an academic democracy. Questions addressed in this section of the project, which spanned 1997-2000, included:

- Gender
- Faculty rank

- Academic discipline
- Task and process orientation
- Communication and writing apprehension
- Motivation for leadership
- Tasks and skills of leadership
- Position stressors
- Leadership style

The majority of these dimensions to the faculty governance unit leader were profiled for survey distribution through existing instruments with some modification. At the conclusion of this line of inquiry, qualitative interview data were gathered to profile leadership styles and to attempt a classification scheme of these leaders. All data collected for this phase of the project were collected between academic years 1996-1999.

Phase III: Topics and Issues Considered

The board believed strongly that the power of a faculty or academic senate can be established by viewing the types and topics of conversations that are undertaken, and eventually, the decisions that these bodies make. The result was a focused three year effort, 1997-2000, to identify what faculty senates were talking about. The approach taken included three dimensions: the scanning and studying of news reports of faculty senate activity, primarily relying on the *Chronicle of Higher Education* for timely reporting of senate activities second, a cross-sectional national survey of faculty governance leaders about topics, and third, an in-depth longitudinal examination of what one faculty senate dealt with over a ten-year period of time.

Impact on Faculty Involvement in Governance

The literature base on faculty involvement in governance is generally vague, with many case study reports and personal narratives populating journals. Foundational work on the topic really occurred just over 30 years ago, but it is firmly rooted in the management literature of the early-1900s. Drawing on a base of Weber

(1947), Taylor (1967), and others, the principal notion is that work environments are improved when authority is shared, and generally efficiency will improve as well. In collective bargaining and many other settings, this is not always the case (Kameras, 1996), as those on the front-line of conducting work are not necessarily the best equipped to make critical decisions. For example, should assembly-line workers be making decisions about financial matters? Probably not, but assembly-line workers might make very good consultants in discussions about space utilization on a factory floor. So, the issue is hardly ever clearly definitive. Such is the case in higher education, as faculty members can provide positive, meaningful input about the nature of the institution without providing definite answers and recommendations.

This general problematic nature of shared authority is a big part of the motivation for the work of the National Data Base on Faculty Involvement in Governance. The project was conceptualized, implemented, and concluded with no formal compensation for any participant, and is as much of a case study in research-teaming and agenda setting as it is about shared authority in higher education.

The implications of the project are substantial, and if applied, have the potential to radically shape how faculty involvement in governance takes place on campuses today. If administrators and faculty alike engage in conversations about expectations and performance, and consensus is achieved, then faculty senates and councils can become powerful forces in defining the campus and the future of higher education. Sadly, though, if institutions continue to be largely reactive rather than active in the decision-making process, administrative power will continue to rise and will potentially eliminate the faculty voice from decision- making. At stake, then, is the notion of academic democracy and the symbolic historical tradition of the collegial campus.

Findings from the project have the potential to impact many different levels of higher education's constituencies. As alluded to earlier, faculty and administrators have a very real and vested interest in how faculty-led decision-making takes place and how administrators respond to shared authority. If administrative growth continues to marginalize faculty involvement, then the pattern of administrative dominance certainly takes center stage. Administrators and governing boards will set curriculum unchecked, make admissions decisions based on criteria they establish, and envision an increasingly corporate-centric university. As discussed earlier, these patterns are clearly evidenced in the treatment of part-time faculty and the envisioning of students who are viewed first and foremost as customers. The result is an incredible value in systematically looking at how administrators see shared governance and critically examining what these faculty decision-making bodies are dealing with today.

The converse perspective is also clearly important to understand. Faculty, as campus citizens have not always consistently demonstrated the disciplined decision-making necessary for building lasting institutional policy. Some will even argue that this lack of responsibility on the part of faculty is at the core of evolving corporate-centered universities. Administrators and policy makers will subsequently find great value in a critical study of faculty involvement in governance.

Students obviously have a great concern for the state of higher education decision-making. Should their curriculum and environment be dictated under the guise of academic freedom or personal career advancement? For the sake of the current and future student populations, this conversation is of the utmost importance. The uneven nature of many program's quality has resulted in increased accreditation by state and national bodies, and these accreditation efforts become not the base of expectation, but rather the goal of academic programs. The accreditation movement in turn impacts a wide number of other programmatic decisions, including which courses to teach, the role and nature of clinical applications, resources to have on hand for student use, and ultimately, which programs get resources, potentially starving other programs in the name of accreditation.

Students are also potentially impacted by curricular decisions and institutional policies that care politically motivated, as in the case of many community college-four-year college articulation agreements. The politicizing of curriculum (and entrance/proficiency exams) demeans the ideals of academic freedom, marginalizes the notion of higher learning, and serves as a motivation for faculty to band together into more formal legal relationships, namely but not exclusively, collective bargaining units.

Yet another body that should have a substantial interest in campus based shared authority are governing board members. Although this relationship is not addressed in the NDBFIG project, the outcomes of the various studies should be of interest and should frame a general policy conversation on decision-making. On most campuses there is marginal faculty representation on a governing board, but this type of representation *de facto* mis-represents the faculty typology, regardless of true representation. The issue of consistency in decision-making is also of interest to board members, as substantially differing views on the process will ultimately create difficulty in both decision inputs and outcomes.

Faculty senates are difficult to generalize, and range widely in power from those that try to close themselves for lack of power (Kellogg, 2001), to those that force a college president's resignation. Most, however, fall somewhere in between on this continuum, and the lack of cataloging and categorization of senates is both surprising and professionally frustrating. The NDBFIG project represents a critical first-step in transcending the radical and philosophical conversations about academic democracy with the business minded approaches to college management that have become a necessity. The value of the conversation, however, is only as real as academic leaders are allowing it to be, that is, faculty must seize the power to gain a voice in the conversation about the future of the university. This power need not be radical sit-ins or a tightly coupled responsiveness with all faculty members, but must include a greater responsiveness to areas where faculty are empowered and must include setting critical agendas. Involvement will only be seen as a management tool while it works, and faculty and administrators alike must find collaborative ways to steward the industry of higher education with care and respect for the ideals of higher learning.

Chapter 4

Faculty Governance Units

Despite an extensive body of literature related to faculty involvement in governance, few generalizations have been undertaken about the role and function of faculty involvement. The most well-known recent study of faculty involvement in governance was undertaken by Gilmour (1991) over a decade ago, with findings that largely reported the existence and use of faculty senates. Indeed, summative findings and reports of faculty senates and councils are common, as are personal narratives about why faculty governance does or does not work (see, for example, Sims, 1998; Baker, 2001).

There are many different types of faculty governance units on campus, with the most traditional being a representative democracy. These "senates" give equal voice to all members, with the possible exception of a conveyor or president, and work on the assumption that members carry information, decisions, ideas, and topics for discussion back to their constituents, usually an academic department or subject matter units. Some colleges make use of assemblies or town halls, where all members of the campus community, either faculty, faculty and staff, or just staff, comprise a body for sounding out issues, taking votes, and making decisions. One faculty council elects representatives by petition-drive, while another takes volunteers on a first-come, first-serve basis. Variations also include executive councils that are appointed by deans, vice presidents, or presidents, bi-cameral legislators with representatives by unit or geographic location and from general elections, faculty representation by rank, and multiple scenarios of staff representation that range from full voting rights for support and administrative staff to standing committees of administrators. Governance units often utilize academic calendars to organize their meetings and programs of work, with many monthly meetings throughout an academic year. Although anecdotal evidence may be common, even the cataloging of how governance units are organized has been relatively neglected, and is an excellent departure point for further research and description.

Flynn (2001) has consulted on how to build effective faculty senates, and has highlighted technical, tangible criteria. He identified such criteria as permanent office space, an annual budget, and an adjusted workload for senate officers. He also stressed the need for symbolic faculty leadership in the rites and rituals of campus life, concluding that the effective senate is holistic in its application to campus. The NDBFIG stream of research on governance units focused on first the role faculty see for themselves in shared governance, what faculty currently see as happening in these bodies at their respective institutions, and what an ideal shared governance unit might look like. From there, the inquiry was then designed to look at college presidents' views of faculty involvement and how college provosts value this involvement.

Baseline NDBFIG Data

The following three sections are all composed of data collected with the baseline NDBFIG survey instrument. The instrument contained 29 questions, and faculty members were asked to respond by rating their level of agreement with each. The first section of the survey asked responding faculty to rate their agreement that the items identified were the current role of faculty in shared governance (five questions). Then, faculty were asked to identify by rating their agreement with both the ideal characteristics (five questions) of a shared governance structure and their agreement with general activities and issues surrounding shared governance (19 questions). As noted in chapter 3, surveys were distributed through centralized contact personnel at individual campuses, and typically involved faculty who had some level of involvement with shared governance activities. Data were collected from 2,491 faculty members out of 3,400 surveyed, for a 73% participation rate.

Faculty Role in Governance

Five items related to how faculty perceived their roles in shared governance. As shown in Table 1, faculty members agreed most strongly with the role that their job is to convince administrators that their voice is valuable in decision-making (mean 4.03). This suggests that faculty do not think that administrators necessarily value their participation in governance, and that suggestion is reinforced with the second highest agreed upon role which was to insist on faculty rights in appropriate settings (mean 3.94). In other words, faculty see their participation as important, and that part of their job is to insist on participating.

Faculty generally agreed that they work harder to cooperate with administrators (mean 3.90), and that they need to work with administrators in the clarification of their roles (mean 3.79). The ratings of these two roles imply that the relationship between faculty members and administrators is certainly civil (e.g., there is an attempt at cooperation), but that there are undertones of an adversarial relationship (e.g., help administrators clarify their job functions). These are consistent with previous reports in the literature base, and allude to an overall environment that has the potential to flare-up as certain issues, personnel, or decisions come into conversation.

Faculty agreed least strongly with the role of involvement in determining budget outcomes (mean 3.47). This is indicative of perhaps one of the biggest problems that shared governance encounters. Budgeting and fiscal oversight are difficult tasks that require an impersonalization and depoliticalization of agendas, or the complete opposite of that neutrality. This is typically where administrative offices have the most difficulty, especially when funding is low or is being reduced. By faculty claiming that this is not their role, administrators will be likely to see (1) that faculty are shying away from a difficult task, and (2) that faculty are not being holistically responsible for the state of the campus. Conversely, faculty may argue that they want to be involved in policy formation, yet many would argue that budgetary evaluation has a great deal to do with policy formation and evaluation.

Table 1
Faculty Roles in Governance*
n=2,491

Role	Mean	SD	n
Convince the administration that the faculty "voice" is a valuable component in decision-making	4.03	.866	2,370
Faculty must insist on rights and responsibilities in appropriate governance roles	3.94	.901	2,271
Faculty committees work harder to cooperate with administration	3.90	.805	2,469
Faculty should assist in clarifying roles of administrators so that they know they are to administer policy and not impose their own	3.79	1.00	2,280
Faculty should be more involved in developing specific outcomes for budgetary expenditures	3.47	1.02	2,273

*Reported on a 1-to-5 Likert-type scale with 1=Strong Disagreement, progressively, to 5=Strong Agreement.

Faculty and Their Involvement

A total of 19 items were included in the section of the survey dealing with faculty perceptions of involvement in governance. Agreement levels ranged from a high of 4.30 (the governance body adequately represents the faculty point of view) to a low of 3.25 (issues considered by the body are not important), with an overall mean rating for all items of 3.74 (see Table 2). Seven of the 19 survey items (36% of the items) had mean ratings of 4.0 or higher, representing agreement by responding faculty. In addition to the high rating of 4.30 for representing the faculty point of view, the following items were rated over 4.0: the governance body practices adhere to the guidelines set forth in its constitution and by-laws (mean 4.20), it is difficult to get people to serve on governance bodies (4.09), the governance body is not well represented on committees making decisions on policy, planning, and allocation of resources (4.08), faculty are not adequately rewarded for their participation (4.01), the governance body operates efficiently (4.00), and the governance body's operating budget is adequate (4.00).

The responses indicated here represent general agreement with the structure of governance bodies, but seems to also reflect a general frustration with pieces of this structure. For example, data confirm that faculty senates represent faculty points of view, are efficient, have the resources to work well, and work in legitimate ways with constitutions and bylaws, but at the same time they have trouble getting people to participate, do not have adequate rewards for participation, and are not well represented on committees that make 'big' decisions.

The next seven items had mean ratings between 3.90 (communication is good between the governance body and academic administrators) and 3.50 (similarity of expectations of the governance body role), representing a range of near consensus agreement to somewhere above (toward agreement) neutral perceptions about the items. Four of these items reinforce the efficiency of the governance unit, as alluded in the previous question. These items include near-agreement level ratings with items about governance body members and academic administrators having good communication (3.90) and meeting regularly (3.82), and having good communications (3.62) and regular meetings (3.69) with board of trustee members. And as indicated, there is a consistency between the expectations of the governance body role between academic administrators and governance body members (3.50). Two items, however, did not reinforce the efficient operation of the governance unit, including the 3.65 mean rating of the governance body not having sufficient information on which to base decisions, and the mean rating of 3.55 indicating a largely neutral perception that the governance body is involved in important decisions about the way the institution is run.

The final five items dealt primarily with the personnel involved in faculty governance. Respondents gave mostly neutral ratings to having no difficulty getting a quorum at meetings (3.48), the governance unit's getting the most capable people involved (3.38), and that the governance body leaders are not well prepared to assume their positions (3.28). The two other items included a neutral perception that the issues considered by the governance body are important (3.25), and that management information is readily provided to the governance body for decision-making (3.38). Interestingly, all of these items are self-referencing and are things that current governance unit members can actively work to address. For example, the AAHE provides a faculty governance training seminar, institutional workshops could also be developed and implemented at a low cost, management information can be obtained through institutional research, and an enthusiasm for attending meetings may be strongly aligned with the types of issues being addressed.

Overall, the ratings of over 2,200 faculty members express some degree of hope and excitement for the future of faculty involvement in governance. Faculty generally agree that the system for shared authority is in place, but seem to be bemoaning the implementation of that system. Much of this can relate to the issues of trust, power sharing, and agenda development, and they are all items within the domain of influence that faculty members can have control over.

Table 2
Faculty Perceptions of Faculty Involvement in Governance
n=2,491

Characteristic	Mean	SD	n
Our governance body adequately represents the faculty point of view	4.30	.966	2,299
Governance body practices adhere to the guidelines set forth in its constitution and bylaws	4.20	.886	2,301
It is difficult to get people to serve on governance body standing and/or ad hoc committees	4.09	.809	2,268

Table 2 *(continued)*
Faculty Perceptions of Faculty Involvement in Governance
n=2,491

Characteristic	Mean	SD	n
Our governance body is not well represented on committees making decisions on policy, planning, and allocation of resources	4.08	.826	2,290
Faculty members are not adequately rewarded for their participation in the governance process	4.01	.858	2,279
The governance body operates efficiently	4.00	.864	2,279
The governance body's operating budget is adequate	4.00	.770	2,278
Communication is good between the governance body and academic administrators	3.90	.850	2,298
Governance body members and academic administrators meet regularly	3.82	.901	2,290
Governance body representatives and the Board of Trustees meet regularly	3.69	.921	2,287
The governance body does not have sufficient information on which to base its decisions	3.65	.970	2,290
Communication is good between the governance body and the Board of Trustees	3.62	1.03	2,291
The governance body is involved in important decisions about the way the institution is run	3.55	.890	2,299
Academic administrators and governance body expectations regarding the governance body's role are the same	3.50	1.01	2,291
We have no difficulty getting a quorum at governance body meetings	3.48	.726	2,011
The governance body attracts the most capable people as members	3.38	.999	2,269
Management information is readily provided to the governance body concerning issues it considers	3.38	.950	2,290
Our governance body leaders are not well prepared to assume their positions	3.28	1.03	2,291
The issues considered by our governance body are not important	3.25	1.02	2,300

Ideal Governance Processes

A total of four items were included on the NDBFIG survey dealing with ideal characteristics of a faculty governance system. These items had been identified in the initial Miller and Seagren (1993) study by a number of faculty senate presidents. Responding faculty agreed most that a faculty governance unit should be utilized as a conduit through which faculty input is solicited (mean 4.12; see Table 3). The implications of an administrative system that does not focus how it illicits faculty input was noted in the follow-up study to NDBFIG activities by Brown and Miller (1997). They reported that minority faculty members in particular felt that the frequent and often uncoordinated solicitation for involvement in campus activities, committees, and governance is a major source of stress and factor in feeling burned out or overwhelmed. Indeed, the lack of coordination of getting faculty involvement can lead to major issues of misrepresentation, burn out, and as can be seen in the senate observations reported in chapter five, can lead to the creation of a culture dominated by a certain sector of faculty who in turn serve as a disincentive to participation.

The use of a senate as a conduit for participation was reinforced by the agreement expressed toward the characteristic of faculty questioning policy through a well articulated process (mean 4.05). This agreement does not necessarily mean that emphasis should be placed on creating more internal policies, such as constitutions and bylaws, but may reflect a larger institutional perspective on how decisions are made. By default, then, there are ramifications concerning the types of issues considered and what topics and types of decisions can be fed into a shared governance system. Subsequent issues of communication and mutual respect can also arise, but faculty seemed to be responding to a basic need for institutional clarity about a decision making process. This was further reinforced by the agreement of faculty toward inclusion early in the decision making process (mean 3.99).

Faculty also agreed (mean 3.99) that in an ideal shared governance system they are adequately rewarded for their participation. There is often a predisposition to think of rewards as equivalent to compensation, however, the emerging national conversation about alternative scholarship suggests that recognition for service can be a powerful reward, and that can and should be considered in the context of involvement with faculty governance.

Responding faculty also agreed somewhat (mean 3.78) that neutral consultants be used to mediate faculty-administrator dealings. The tone of the item suggests the use of collective bargaining units or union involvement, and the rise in union membership supports the agreement level. The use of unions, however, is but one form of mediation, as any number of formal and informal mediators could be possible, ranging from offices of human resources providing assistance in hiring equity or coordinating merit pay processes, to formal arbitration boards. The agreement level, though, suggests that faculty do indeed see room for third party involvement as they deal with administrators, but that this involvement may be temporal or situational.

Table 3
Characteristics of an Ideal Co-Governance Process
N=2,491

Characteristic	Mean	SD	n
The faculty senate is utilized as a conduit through which faculty participation is solicited	4.12	.780	2,269
Faculty are empowered to question policy decisions through well articulated process	4.05	.699	2,251
Faculty members are adequately rewarded for their participation in the governance process	3.99	.880	2,271
Institutional procedures involve faculty governance early in the decision-making process	3.99	.900	2,270
Neutral "consultants" are utilized to mediate faculty-administration dealings	3.78	.823	2,254

College Presidents and Faculty Involvement

Scroggs (1949) outlined the most basic tenet of college administration: "the president is the board's administrative agent through whom the college is operated" (p. 443). A fundamental precept of meaningful shared governance is the respect and authority given to the process by the college president. From this direction, subsequent offices and administrators will follow the institutional leadership to cultivate and respect the faculty role in governance or to give the process only cursory consideration. Governance broadly, encompassing those sets of behaviors that share power, create policy, and allocate resources, has multiple layers of decision-making and importance. College presidents must determine their own reasoning, assess their campus' climate and culture, and determine to what extent and how they will involve faculty in decision-making. This involvement and the identification of the amount of involvement is a political process that by its very definition can create problems on campus, among a public and among governing boards. Therefore, how presidents view faculty involvement in governance was included in the NDBFIG line of inquiry. Specifically, college presidents were asked "what is your perspective, as a college president, on the value of faculty involvement in governance?"

The project encompassing the presidential perspective was intended to be exploratory and descriptive in nature, and the Delphi survey technique was selected as an appropriate methodology. The Delphi survey technique allows for the creation of consensus among geographically separated experts, allows for an equal participation among the sample, and provides participants an opportunity for reflection.

In 2000, a random sample of 30 college presidents was selected based on institutional identification, and using a table of random numbers, for inclusion in the study. A total of 23 of the 30 (76%) college presidents completed all three rounds of the Delphi survey. In the initial round of the survey, presidents reported a wide variety of written comments that were distilled into 20 basic statements about their perspectives on faculty involvement in governance. Approximately 17 statements developed by college presidents were considered duplicated and were combined into the 20 to be rated in the second and third round of the Delphi survey. During the second round of the survey, respondents had an overall mean rating of the 20 items of 2.31. In the third round of the survey, the participating college presidents changed a total of 18 initial ratings (averaging fewer than one per participant) with a resulting increase in the overall mean rating to 2.40. Over half of the mean ratings of the presidentially developed perceptions fell within the 2.50 to 3.00 range, indicating strong levels of agreement. The participating presidents rated a vigorous defense of academic freedom (mean 2.91, SD .288) and the essential nature of faculty governance in curriculum development (mean 2.91, SD .288) the highest (see Table 4). Also very strongly rated by presidents was the argument that faculty should focus more on teaching and less on institutional management (mean 2.87, SD .458), and that there is a need for the president to take a leadership role in faculty involvement in governance (mean 2.85, SD .359). Conversely, presidents agreed least with the argument that faculty governance increases commitment to the mission of the university (mean 1.65, SD .714). Presidents also tended to disagree with the notion that faculty feel the impact of policy decisions more then other constituencies due to their proximity to students (mean 1.82, SD .717), and that faculty governance is vital to an institution (mean 1.87, SD .920). On this last perception, nearly half of the responding presidents (n=11; valid 48%) indicated that they disagreed that faculty governance was vital by rating it "Disagree." Similarly, there was neither strong agreement or disagreement with the statement "I strongly support faculty governance" (mean 2.00, SD .905), although 39% (valid) of the presidents disagreed with the notion.

College presidents have an interest in how faculty are involved in governance issues, but that interest need not be unabashed enthusiasm and support. By identifying 20 unique aspects of how college presidents view shared governance, they provide a solid framework for framing various decision-making roles on campus. For example, one view of shared faculty governance allows for a system of checks and balances with college administrators, yet their study respondents seem to frame the work of faculty as related to curriculum, and extend far enough to discourage faculty governance in institutional management.

What is perhaps most striking about these study findings is the view that college presidents in fact do not blindly support faculty involvement in governance. Indeed, presidential ratings plainly spell out a perspective that shared governance is not an integral component of institutional decision-making and management. In fact, the very opposite seems to be suggested, and this idea is quite counter to much of the existing literature base. The result is the need for a broad, general study of college presidents and how they interact with faculty governance bodies. Only in doing so will institutions and all of their assorted parts be capable of streamlining effective decision-making and performing at levels of sophistication that can withstand any and all public (and private) accountability inquiries.

Table 4
Presidential Mean Rating of Perceptions of Faculty Involvement in Governance
N=30

Perception	Mean	Mode	SD
Presidents should vigorously defend the value of academic freedom	.2.91	3.00	.288
Faculty involvement in governance is essential in curriculum development.	2.91	3.00	.288
Faculty focus should be more on teaching and less on institutional management.	2.87	3.00	.458
There still is a need for the president to take a leadership role in faculty involvement in governance.	2.85	3.00	.359

Table 4 *(continued)*
Presidential Mean Rating of Perceptions of Faculty Involvement
in Governance
N=30

Perception	Mean	Mode	SD
We need to work with faculty on a common set of values.	2.82	3.00	.388
Faculty governance has a tradition in curricular issues.	2.78	3.00	.422
A college's success in achieving its mission and objectives relies on faculty support and participation in governance.	2.73	3.00	.449
Faculty have a conflict of interest with governance. A separation of powers and responsibilities is appropriate.	2.63	3.00	.581
Presidential leadership is most effective when faculty support is marshaled.	2.60	3.00	.656
Presidents should be the only report to the official governing body.	2.56	3.00	.507
Collaborative leadership invites input and dialogue.	2.56	3.00	.662
Faculty governance is limited to observer-participant for understanding and communication, but not for full governance.	2.30	3.00	.765
Faculty involvement in governance increases the level of awareness among faculty.	2.27	2.00	.703
Those who help create will also support.	2.08	2.00	.793
Faculty governance is absolutely crucial if there is to be buy-in.	2.00	2.00	.739
I strongly support faculty governance.	2.00	1.00	.905

Table 4 *(continued)*
Presidential Mean Rating of Perceptions of Faculty Involvement
in Governance
N=30

Perception	Mean	Mode	SD
Faculty governance increases their commitment to the university.	1.91	2.00	.668
Faculty governance is vital to the institution.	1.87	1.00	.920
Because faculty typically have the greatest influence on and interaction with students, they recognize and experience the impact of policy decisions as significantly as, and often more so than, any constituency group in an institution.	1.82	2.00	.717
Faculty governance increases their commitment to the mission of the university.	1.65	1.00	.714

How Provosts Value Faculty Involvement

The primary area that faculty members believe they have a "right" to in governance is the curriculum. As an area of responsibility for the provost or vice president for academic affairs, an important aspect to understanding how faculty involvement works is how the provost values shared governance. The role of the provost in faculty-led decision-making has primarily been explored through personal narratives, anecdotal commentaries, and some best practice reporting. A provost must rely on a board to delineate responsibility to campus administrators, and the provost subsequently plays an important role either serving as the front line of senior administration, conveying the will of the president and board, or alternatively, as a form of faculty whip, mustering faculty support and introducing new ideas and initiatives.

The vice president for academic affairs, also commonly referred to as "provost," has direct responsibility for faculty, curriculum, and degree programs. Increasingly, these administrators have responsibility for student affairs issues, enrollment services, articulation agreements, institutional assessment, and in some instances, international delivery of programs. Despite the broad menu of areas of work, the academic offerings, the pedagogy, and content of the institution are the primary domains of the provost. Hence, if faculty are chiefly concerned with curricular issues, their primary administrative interface will be with a provost.

As early as 1870, Charles W. Eliot, president of Harvard, appointed the first "dean" to relieve himself of some of the burdens of administration. This individual would be an active faculty member who would also serve in an administrative capacity (Eliot, 1908). With this new delineation of responsibilities, as well as with higher education becoming more complex and serving more students, the dean of the college has become even more prevalent. One of the driving reasons for this emergence has been due to the evolving president's role, as the president has become more of an external officer (Birnbaum, 1992), while the dean has become the internal leader of the campus.

The dean of the college or academic dean is now a significant part of every institution with various names used to identify the position. As early as the 1960s the title "provost" was used to identify the individual who filled the position, while state-supported colleges and universities have used 'vice president for academic affairs' or 'academic vice president.'

Gould (1968) found that a majority of provosts had no formal training in administration, had stopped teaching, and had no experience when they were appointed. The pathway to the provost has changed somewhat, as experience in department chair and decanal positions now seem virtually mandatory. The provost has been compared to the mythical "argus" with many eyes that are always alert and able to react at any given time, considering the complex nature of the position and its interactions with various constituents including the institution's president, governing boards, deans, and others. Generally, there has been wide recognition that the position has changed (Martin, Samels, & Associates, 1997)

The extent to which a provost makes use of a faculty governance unit varies greatly. The rationale for inclusion of faculty senates in the work of the provost can include the generation of new and exciting ideas, building support for new programs or initiatives, and creating a sense of ownership among faculty for decision-making results (Rosovsky, 1990). The reliance on faculty to make decisions, however, implies an investment of power to faculty. This construct of faculty co-governance is not broadly accepted. Aronowitz (2000) noted of the evolving nature of the college campus that "Öfaculty feel like employees rather than members of communities devoted to common intellectual concerns" (p. 67). This change in mindset has come largely due to a corporate model being imposed on the idea of a college, that faculty "[I]n consideration of their new, proletarianized status, many have joined unions and converted their faculty senates into adversarial bodies" (p. 67).

The relationship between faculty, the provost, and ultimately the college president begins to resemble, then, the political structure of a state-federal government relationship. While a national leader has ultimate authority on a set of issues, the state-level leader has many more operational responsibilities. The analogy, then, holds that a provost resembles a state governor, responsible for the implementation of work and rewards necessary for the institution to operate.

As an exploratory study of the provost position and faculty senates, a Delphi survey was utilized with a purposive sample of 20 provosts in the 2000-2001 academic year. The provosts were selected from liberal arts colleges (n=10) and research focused universities (n=10). Criteria for selection were (1) geographic diversity, (2) the institution's use of a faculty senate as evidenced by a publicly-accessible website, and (3) a willingness to participate once the institution was identified.

The initial survey was mailed to the sample of provosts in the fall semester of 2000. The questions for the provosts to respond to was "what is your perspective, as provost, on the value of faculty involvement in governance?" After all 20 round one surveys were received, all responses were separated into individual ideas, totaling 34 items. After eliminating for duplication, 20 items remained to be rated in the second round of the Delphi survey. In the second round, participants were asked to rate their agreement with each item so that a rating of 3 would mean that they agreed that the statement was an accurate, true, and important component of the value of faculty involvement in governance. A rating of 2 indicated neither agreement nor disagreement, and a 1 indicated disagreement with the statement. Using follow-up telephone calls and email messages, all 20 participants responded to the second and third rounds of the survey.

After completion of data collection, mean scores were computed for each survey item. For the liberal arts institution provosts, 10 items were rated with a mean score of 2.8 or higher on the 3-point Likert-type scale. These provosts provided an overall mean rating of 2.71 for all 20 items, and had six items that were rated a "3" by all ten provosts (see Table 5). This complete consensus was noted on the following perspectives: governance implies shared ownership, faculty focus should be on teaching, scholarship, and advising, good faculty involvement actually spreads the workload around and allows more work to get done, faculty governance is more essential now than ever, faculty involvement increases understanding of university strengths and weaknesses, and faculty involvement strengthens democratic principles at work.

Collectively, this consensus alludes to an attention to the functions and content of shared governance units, and implies that communication, while essential, is not guaranteed to be two-way. The high rating of items, though, does reflect an environment or culture, from the perspective of the provost, that faculty involvement in governance is important and is part of the institutional fabric. This is perhaps best reflected in the complete consensus on perspective about faculty governance being more important now than ever before.

Provosts from research-oriented universities rated 11 of the items as 2.8 or higher, had an overall mean rating for the 20 items of 2.66, and three of the items had complete consensus as evidenced by a rating of 3 by all ten provosts. Overall, the 20 items were given a mean rating of 2.69, with seven items having a mean rating of 2.8 or higher. The complete consensus items for these provosts were: faculty buy-in is essential to policies being effectively implemented, faculty governance has a tradition in curricular issues, and faculty involvement strengthens democratic principles at work. The implication from these ratings is that research-oriented university provosts see faculty governance as a functionary process that has a role in decision-making, largely curricular, and while there may not be an implicit tight coupling in decision-making, involvement does have the potential for a positive effect on the institution.

Three significant differences were identified between the mean ratings of items between the provosts at liberal arts and research-oriented universities, with the liberal arts provosts rating two of the three items higher. Research institution provosts agreed more strongly that faculty governance is necessary for a sense of fairness (2.90 mean as compared to 2.30 mean) than liberal arts provosts. Liberal arts provosts agreed more strongly that faculty focus should be on teaching, scholarship, and advising, and faculty governance is more essential now then ever (3.0 for both as compared to 2.3 and 2.3, respectively).

The roles and responsibilities of the provost have developed and increased exponentially since the early origins of the position in the late nineteenth century. The provost position, with broad responsibilities for the academic welfare of the institution, is now significant in daily operations at many institutions due to the increased necessity of the president to serve in an external capacity. Despite their origins and in some cases present status as faculty members, the provost's administrative decisions do not necessarily represent those of the faculty as a whole. This reality makes it important to understand their perceptions of how and why faculty should be involved in the governance process. This study explored the perspectives of these leaders from institutions with two distinct types of missions to determine their notions of shared governance.

Provosts reported high levels of agreement that faculty governance is important to an institution. Although the type of institution a provost works at may have some bearing on how they view faculty-led decision-making, the differences were minimal, but were reflected in the general nature of responses. Collectively, this consensus alludes to an attention to the functions and content of shared governance units, and implies that communication, while essential, is not guaranteed to be two-way. The high rating of items, though, does reflect an environment or culture, from the perspective of the provost, that faculty involvement in governance is important and is part of the institutional fabric. This is perhaps best reflected in the complete consensus on the perspective regarding faculty governance being more important now than ever before. Largely, liberal arts provosts viewed shared decision-making as a cultural reflection of an institution, while research-oriented university provosts tended to view shared governance as a tool for decision-making. These differences were subtle in the context of the current study, and certainly are in need of further extrapolation.

Liberal arts provosts also seemed to value the participation of faculty members in the governance process to spread the workload. At many of their institutions, which typically are smaller than the research institutions, the necessity for this type of activity is significant in accomplishing duties and making decisions where administrators are limited. This also promotes another statement that this group of provosts rated highly, which was shared ownership.

Perhaps one of the strongest findings of the study was the identification that provosts view faculty involvement as a mechanism for strengthening democratic principles at work. There was total consensus from both groups of provosts regarding this statement. This is significant in light of faculty mistrust of administrators (Birnbaum, 1992). Despite their apparent detachment from the desires of the faculty due to their administrative roles, this demonstrates that provosts continue to appreciate the concept of shared governance. If higher education truly has an empowering history of social justice, then the notion of shared governance is certainly consistent with reinforcing that history.

Table 5
Provost's Perspective on the Value of Faculty Involvement in Governance
N=20

Perspective	Liberal Arts Mean (SD)	Research Mean (SD)	Overall Mean (SD)	f prob
Faculty governance is almost a redundancy.	1.60 (.516)	1.50 (.707)	1.55 (.604)	.722
Faculty involvement in governance is absolutely essential.	2.60 (.516)	2.60 (.699)	2.60 (.598)	1.000
Faculty buy-in is essential to policies being effectively implemented.	2.70 (.483)	3.00 (.000)	2.85 (.366)	.0652
Governance implies shared ownership.	3.00 (.000)	2.80 (.421)	2.90 (.307)	.1510
Mission of the institution \moves forward because of shared ownership.	2.60 (.516)	2.40 (.843)	2.50 (.688)	.5305
Faculty governance is absolutely crucial if there is to be buy-in to policy outcomes.	2.80 (.421)	2.80 (.421)	2.80 (.410)	1.000
Faculty governance is necessary for a sense of fairness.	2.30 (.823)	2.90 (.316)	2.60 (.680)	.0453*
Faculty governance has a tradition in curricular issues.	2.80 (.421)	3.00 (.000)	2.90 (.307)	.1510
Faculty involvement in governance is essential in curriculum development.	2.70 (.483)	2.80 (.421)	2.75 (.444)	.6278
Being the core of the university setting, faculty governance is central to broader institutional decision-making.	2.60 (.699)	2.90 (.316)	2.75 (.550)	.2323
Faculty governance is most effective in the area of academic program development.	2.80 (.421)	2.80 (.632)	2.80 (.523)	1.000

Table 5
Provost's Perspective on the Value of Faculty Involvement in Governance
N=20

Perspective	Liberal Arts Mean (SD)	Research Mean (SD)	Overall Mean (SD)	f prob
Faculty focus should be on teaching, scholarship, and advising.	3.00 (.000)	2.30 (.674)	2.65 (.587)	.0042*
Faculty should be consulted during decision-making processes to add perspective.	2.70 (.483)	2.60 (.516)	2.65 (.489)	.6601
Good faculty involvement actually spreads the workload around and allows more work to get done.	3.00 (.000)	2.80 (.421)	2.90 (.307)	.1510
Faculty governance is more essential now than ever.	3.00 (.000)	2.30 (.674)	2.65 (.587)	.0042
We need to work with faculty on a common set of values.	2.70 (.483)	2.60 (.516)	2.65 (.489)	.6601
Faculty governance is valuable because it offers an opportunity to make an investment in the institution.	2.80 (.632)	2.60 (.516)	2.70 (.571)	.4486
Faculty involvement in governance increases the level of awareness among faculty.	2.60 (.699)	2.70 (.483)	2.65 (.587)	.7142
Faculty involvement in governance increases understanding of university strengths and weaknesses.	3.00 (.000)	2.90 (.316)	2.95 (.223)	.3306
Faculty involvement in governance strengthens democratic principles at work.	3.00 (.000)	3.00 (.000)	3.00 (.000)	.5443

*significant at the .05 level.

Impact on Faculty Involvement in Governance

Despite their wide variety of forms, this phase of the NDBFIG project attempted to catalog some of the perceptions held about shared governance bodies and activities using national samples. The findings begin to outline several national trends and depict an increasingly politically-charged environment for the higher education community.

The first section of findings, reporting faculty perceptions about faculty involvement in governance, depict a somewhat self-serving view of the faculty senate. They reported that while their decisions or activities are not well respected, they do indeed represent their colleagues well, are efficient, have an adequate budget, and abide by appropriate rules and procedures. They also seem to indicate a desire to play a larger role in assigning faculty work, as evidenced by their desire to be a conduit for committee work and assignments. Conversely, though, they did notice an inability to get good people involved in faculty governance, and that they do not have enough representation on key committees.

While these general findings do reflect some self-satisfaction, taken at face value they indicate a need for a more focused vision from senior administrators. Presidents and provosts need to see these governance units as positive bodies that can be high performing, valuable assets to charting the course of the institution.

Presidential responses stressed the value of academic freedom, and suggested that faculty should spend less time on institutional management and more time on teaching. However, they also indicated that they are essential to curriculum development, and that the president's role should be more active in leading them. Again, on face value, presidents look supportive of shared governance and seem to be charging them to focus on curricular (however that may be defined) decisions and issues. Provosts similarly recognized the tradition of faculty involvement in curriculum management, and expanded that support to academic program development. Perhaps most importantly, though, from the provost's perspective faculty involvement is vital to policy development. Further, provosts reported that faculty involvement in governance implies shared governance and that its use strengthens democratic principles.

Data suggest an environment ripe for change and perhaps greater or more efficient utilization of governance bodies. No major structural barriers were identified as prohibiting better use of representative democracies, and the biggest barrier coming out of the responses were attitudinal differences, differing expectations, and cultural traditions. For governance bodies to assume greater responsibility, they must break through to administrators and their fellow faculty to earn the respect they believe they deserve. The obvious barrier of not being able to get good people to serve on the faculty governance unit may be somewhat self-reinforcing, and the notion of a conduit may prove to be powerful. Brown and Miller (1998) found, for example, that many minority faculty members felt abused and were asked too often to serve on committees and the like to represent multi-ethnic points of view. Some campuses make use of committees on committees, and such a structure remanded to a faculty senate, if handled well, could invigorate a governance body. Similarly, if both presidents and provosts see curricular matters as the primary responsibility, governance bodies have a tremendous opportunity to demonstrate their abilities and value to virtually all institutional bodies, especially if curricular and academic matters include enrollment management issues and concerns.

Presidents and provosts seem to be in a position of power with an ability to infuse success in governance bodies. This is consistent with the presidential notion that they should take a leadership role in faculty involvement in governance.

There may also be a subtext to the data, though, meaning that the responses reflect more of a political correctness than the reality of shared governance. The emerging corporate mindset of the university coupled with unprecedented administrative strength has, in many settings, created a dichotomous political environment where faculty might feel unwilling or unable to concede that governance strategies do not work or are not effective. This creates a general cautionary note for all research on shared governance and academic senates, much like the caution necessary in dealing with generalizations in any democratic or elected society.

If indeed there is an over-reporting in favor of shared governance, the action itself demonstrates something of a desire to support senates and other bodies who attempt to claim the rights of faculty members. By reporting what would be considered most appropriate or "best" on the part of faculty, respondents might be attempting to protect their own self-interests and not concede dissatisfaction with the status quo.

Whether intentional or authentic, the display or response by faculty members does demonstrate a proximity to power that could be defined as a political party rather than a political structure. The idealistic behavior on the part of faculty who are unwilling to compromise offers an intensity of belief that can at times be a barrier to the political deal making and bargaining that are often required for a political body to be effective. Further, the purity of beliefs by some faculty members, particularly those with long institutional histories who may see new waves of administrators as fads, may prove to be incapable of developing collections of interests (interest aggregation) to obtain power to seriously challenge these administrators.

As indicated by the responses, however, the relationship between faculty and administrators is not entirely adversarial, and responses further suggest that the parties involved generally want to make the system of shared authority effective. A strong line of inquiry emerging from the NDBFIG project, then, is the need to classify and report specific strategies for improving the relationships between faculty and administrators, and to offer serious training and long-term education about how democratic enterprises can be effectively managed and worked within the larger context of a democratic institution. There are very subtle differences in this distinction, namely the overarching governing board that has the power to be autocratic in decision-making.

Training will not be successful if labeled "training for faculty senate success," yet such a title could be an effective beginning to a long-term, multi-faceted campaign. Elements of such a campaign might include re-conceptualized faculty senate training that focuses more on democratic behaviors (communication, education, etc.) and less on the structure of specific senates. For administrators, long-term educational efforts might include more reports of best-practice or benchmarks, demonstrations of how senates and other bodies help shape success in various offices, the provision of office and technical support, and efforts to develop a cooperative attitude by both administrators and faculty that is not based on concession, but rather, compromise.

Chapter 5

Faculty Governance Leaders

Although the body of literature and contemporary thinking about shared governance has worked in ebbs and flows, little attention has historically been placed on those faculty leaders who assume positions of responsibility within faculty governance organizations. These faculty members are the ones who commit tremendous amounts of time and energy to the broad objectives of advancing the institution and defending faculty rights. The temptations, however, can be difficult to resist. Some faculty who assume these leadership roles find themselves whisked away to football and basketball games, dinners in presidential mansions, frequent catered meetings with senior college and university administrators, private clerical support, private offices that far exceed that of most faculty, and even reserved parking, meal passes, theater tickets, and priority scheduling of classrooms. How faculty can hold true to their constituents without succumbing to the trappings of power is one challenge that badly needs to be addressed, and the NDBFIG project attempted to initiate some of the conversation about faculty in leadership positions in senates and similar governance bodies.

The key to faculty governance units is the lead, elected or appointed faculty member who has the ability to provide group direction. The successful faculty leader can muster support for issues, find and enlist the support of strong, capable, and talented faculty, and can look to the future by developing a pipeline of future faculty senators or representatives. The faculty leader provides the pace, tenor, and tone of the faculty senate or governance body, and by individual behavior, defines the group as being active or reactive, progressive or isolationist, and willing or unwilling to take risks. These leaders also have the potential to demonstrate and profess the extent to which group decisions are accepted and to what extent the governance body provides a meaningful recommendation or challenge to the decision-making process and outcome. Governance leaders are *de facto* the voice and face of the senates, councils, and units that they represent. As such, there are some, although not many, training opportunities for them. The National Education Association, for example, has provided a pre-conference workshop for senate leaders, but few other opportunities exist.

Many colleges and universities that offer faculty senates or similar bodies also provide brief orientations to service on a faculty senate. These orientations are typically brief and provide cursory information on making the transition to senate (or unit) service or leadership. A sample listing of topics covered at one orientation included: history of the senate, orientation to senate resources and facilities, review of senate constitution and Robert's Rules of Order, review of committee charges and responsibilities, and concluded with an executive committee meeting. This one-day training provided no discussion of leadership or communication, nothing about setting priorities and handling stress, and nothing about relating to administrators and fellow faculty while serving in an elected position. There is a tremendous need for serious training about how to operate senate (or unit) business in an efficient and productive manner while still maintaining the academic orientation that roots faculty involvement in governance with the faculty.

Profiling Governance Leaders

Profiling the demographic characteristics of governance leaders can be valuable for a number of reasons. By determining the characteristics and primary identifiers of faculty governance unit leaders, a better understanding of the behaviors of the organizations can be achieved, along with developing strategies for improving individual and organizational behaviors. This component of NDBFIG research was guided largely by the notion that two- and four-year colleges and universities have substantial, inherent differences in roles, responsibilities, and external governance, so the NDBFIG project initially allowed for the stratification of governance leaders along these institutional types. The first effort was subsequently designed to profile governance leaders and how they generally viewed their work.

Profile of 4-Year Faculty Governance Leaders

The ability of a faculty senate or similar governance unit to effectively function has been noted by both scholars and practitioners alike, yet the value of the organization to serve as a forum for debate has also been noted (Baldridge, 1982; Birnbaum, 1988). The key to these governance units, however, is the lead, elected, or appointed faculty member who has the ability to provide group direction.

As an exploratory study, the current effort made use of a stratified random sample of faculty senate leaders at three types of colleges and universities: research and doctoral institutions, comprehensive colleges and university and liberal arts colleges, and community and junior colleges. As no major collective clearinghouse on faculty governance offers a listing of senate or unit leaders, institutions were selected for study based on their Carnegie Classification, and subsequent efforts were made to identify faculty senate leaders. As a cautionary note, not all institutions made use of a faculty senate, and in those instances a lead faculty member was identified from the representative group (chair of the faculty council, chair of the faculty forum, lead professor, etc.), or the survey was mailed to the dean of the faculty or academic affairs with a request that the survey be forwarded to the leader of the faculty governance group.

A total of 300 institutions were identified for participation in the study, with 100 drawn from each cell. Each faculty leader was mailed a survey instrument in early fall 1998, and one follow-up mailing was utilized to increase the response rate. A total of 223 surveys were ultimately returned for inclusion in the data analysis, representing a 74% overall response rate. These respondents represented 76 research or doctoral granting universities (76% of the identified cell), 64 comprehensive universities and liberal arts colleges (64% of the cell), and 83 community can junior colleges (83% of the cell).

Table 6
Demographic Profile of Faculty Governance Leaders
N=223

Characteristic	Research n=76%/n		Comp & LA n=64 %/n		Com Col n=83 %/n		Overall N=223	%/N
Gender								
Male	34	44%	21	32%	63	76%	118	53%
Female	42	55	43	67	20	24	105	47
Rank								
Assistant	7	9%	3	4%	15	18%	25	11%
Associate	31	41	18	29	14	17	63	28
Professor	27	36	39	61	15	18	81	36
Other	9	12	2	3	37	45	48	21
N/R	2	2	2	2	2	2	6	3
Discipline								
Liberal Arts	22	29%	26	40%	48	58%	96	43%
Business	0	0	7	11	3	3	10	4
Agriculture	0	0	0	0	8	10	8	3
Education	2	2	2	2	0	0	4	2
Engineering	5	7	3	5	1	1	9	4
Law	4	5	0	0	0	0	4	2
Medicine	7	10	14	22	0	0	21	9
Social Work	0	0	0	0	0	0	0	0
Commtns	14	19	9	14	7	8	30	13
Other	22	29	3	4	16	20	41	18
Orientation								
Task	43	56%	41	64%	32	38%	116	52%
Process	33	43	23	36	51	61	107	48

As shown in Table 6, the majority of respondents were male (53%), with most identifying their faculty rank as Full Professor (36%), who taught in the Liberal Arts (43%). The finding is somewhat deceiving, as females held the majority of leadership positions in the governance units in both research and comprehensive universities and liberal arts colleges, while males held a three-to-one advantage in the community colleges. Faculty rank in the community college, however, was more evenly distributed with the exception of 45% of the respondents who indicated a rank of "other," probably a result of the use of instructor or general "faculty" titles in many community, junior, and technical colleges. Associate Professors outnumbered Full Professors by a slim margin in research universities (41% to 36%), but Full Professors held the faculty leadership positions at 61% of the comprehensive universities and liberal arts colleges. Overall, few assistant professors held the leadership position (overall 11%), although 18% of the faculty leaders in the community college held the assistant professor title.

For academic disciplines, the majority of respondents represented the Liberal Arts overall (43%) and at each category of institution, with the exception of the research university, where an equal number of respondents came from the "other" category (29% in each). A total of 41 respondents overall came from other disciplines, such as communications (n=30; 13%) and medicine (n=21; 9%) where the next largest disciplines were represented.

The majority of faculty governance unit leaders perceived themselves to be task oriented (n=116; 52%) as compared to process oriented (n=107, 48%). This majority was consistent at research universities (task orientation, n=43, 56%) and in the responses from leaders at comprehensive colleges and universities and liberal arts colleges (n=41, 64%). Community college faculty leaders, however, were primarily process oriented (n=51; 61%)

Included in the survey instrument were the Personal Report of Communication Apprehension (PRCA), developed by McCroskey in the late-1960s, and the Writing Apprehension Test (WAT), developed by Daly and Miller. Both instruments are common measures of communication reticence, with the PRCA dealing with oral communication. The PRCA consists of 24-items, and has a hypothetical mid-point of 75. High communication apprehension, an indicator of lower self-perceptions and self-confidence, is indicated on the instrument with a score of 88 or higher. Low communication apprehension, as indicated by a score below 62, is an indicator of increased satisfaction with formal education, effective public speaking, opportunities for discussion, and so on. The Writing Apprehension Test (WAT), comprised of 20 items, is a measure of apprehension, anxiety, or fear of writing. WAT scores range from 20 to 100, with scores below 45 indicating low levels of apprehension, and over 75 indicating high levels of apprehension. There are many excellent explanations and discussions of communication apprehension, such as those by McCroskey (1977), McCroskey and Sheahan (1978), and Richmond and McCroskey (1989).

Table 7
Communication Apprehension Levels of Faculty Governance Leaders by Institution Type

Institution Type	Mean Scores	
	PRCA (range) n=223	WAT (range) n=221
Research	66.09 (43-71)	60.40 (40-80)
Comprehensive/ Liberal Arts	68.64 (50-84)	57.53 (40-78)
Community College	70.87 (60-79)	61.96 (42-79)
Average	68.53	60.14

Faculty governance leaders participating in the study had an overall PRCA score of 68 and WAT score of 60, indicating that leaders had moderate levels of apprehension for both oral and written communication encounters. As shown in Table 7, community college faculty governance leaders had the highest oral communication apprehension level at a mean score of 70, followed by comprehensive university and liberal arts faculty leaders with an average of 68. Comprehensive university and liberal arts college faculty leaders, however, had the lowest writing apprehension level with a mean score of 57, followed by research university faculty with a mean score of 60.

Faculty governance leaders fell within one standard deviation of the hypothetical mid-points of both the PRCA and the WAT, indicating moderate, situational apprehension about oral communication encounters and writing episodes. For all three groups of faculty, communication apprehension levels were identified in the moderate to normal range, an indication that many of these leaders may well be serving out of a sense of responsibility and professional obligation rather than out of a desire to pursue a specific communication-based agenda (for instance, seeking charisma-based power and influence over the body).

The governance leaders in the study overall displayed a moderate level of apprehension for oral communications. These leaders, like most elected officials, tend to exemplify good oral interpersonal skills when they are among colleagues and friends. However, the true nature and potential for success a faculty governance leader depends upon is the ability of the person to interact with various constituencies, especially senior administrators and among faculty colleagues. Considering the recent relationship between faculty and senior administrators, it is essential that both of these groups work to eliminate or reduce barriers to communication. The most obvious way to improve this oral communication seems to be the inclusion of members from both groups in faculty meetings and also senior level institutional meetings. Inclusion opens the lines of communication, while also providing both groups the opportunity to participate in each others' planning and decision-making processes. A mediator or facilitator may be needed initially to ensure the development of trust and equality of individual group ideas.

Study findings revealed interesting conceptual thinking about how faculty governance leaders perceive their roles. The majority of faculty senate presidents and chairs viewed their role as being task-oriented, that is, dealing with specific program of work items or themes throughout the course of a term. These terms, although common in areas such as political science and public administration, do not accurately convey whether these governance unit leaders viewed their role as instigators of institutional policy reform. A nearly equal number of leaders were process-oriented, indicating that they viewed their leadership role as one of facilitating the operation of a faculty co-governance unit. This process might include setting agendas, scheduling meeting rooms, providing minutes of meetings, updating unit web pages, processing paper work related to attendance, and so forth. Few NDBFIG efforts overall have been able to identify the curious characteristics which set apart active faculty governance unit leaders, and those who see their term in office as "filling time." Future research must begin to address how these presidents and chairs take on active roles in supporting the faculty position in opposition or support of institutional administration.

The immediate applications for these findings are in the transitional efforts of faculty governance units, and how leaders share or transcend the expectations for leadership among and to each other. For faculty co-governance to be effective in the future, leadership must be seen as an opportunity to provide direction and overall enthusiasm for the work of the co-governance unit, and this leadership needs to be nurtured with the immediate president or chair, and transcended to others in preparation for their succession. Leadership needs to be cultivated in an environment where real expectations are placed on senators and representatives so that the entire governance body works collectively to advance a common agenda. As background literature has demonstrated, the process of shared governance has not been widely studied, and this alone may be problematic for future leaders. Those in positions of influence within academic affairs must take on a more aggressive leadership style to create an environment where election to the highest position of representation among faculty is heralded and supported.

Skills and Stress

A second study of faculty governance unit leaders in four-year colleges was conducted between the academic years of 1998-2000. A random sample of 300 faculty senates were again identified first based on institutional name using a traditional guide/directory to four-year higher education institutions. A second level of identification was conducted by identifying the exact faculty senate leader at each of those 300 institutions. A variation from the first study was the decision not to stratify the sample based on institutional type, allowing for a broader discussion of findings rather than on particular cells of faculty leaders. A total of 199 (66%) surveys were ultimately returned, but due to either respondent markings or non-completed survey instruments, 181 were determined to be usable in the current data analysis (60% usable response rate). The survey utilized Seagren, et. al.'s (1994) listing of the 11 skills needed for academic administration and Gmelch and Burn's (1994) identification of 13 faculty stressors. For each listing, faculty governance unit leaders were asked to rate their strong agreement (5) to strong disagreement (1; with 3=neither agreement or disagreement) with each item's applicability to themselves. For the skills section, faculty were asked to rate each item considering the following: This skill is necessary for me to be an effective faculty senate leader.

Four of the eleven skills had overall mean ratings of 4.0 or higher, indicating that the group of responding faculty senate presidents agreed to strongly agreed that the skill was necessary for presiding over a faculty senate. The overall mean rating for all eleven items was 3.80, indicating a perception that the skills were perceived to have a neutral importance to some importance. The highest mean rating was given to the skill of oral communication skills (mean 4.26), followed by leadership skills (4.10), organizational ability (4.06), and stress tolerance (4.00). Three of the items had low-neutral ratings between 3.0 and 3.5, including range of interests (3.48), educational values (3.4), and sensitivity (3.39). The remaining four skills had ratings that fell between 3.66 and 3.82.

The stressors included on the survey instrument were identified by Gmelch as activities or situations that produce unhealthy or unwelcome stress for an individual in higher education. Using a modified Likert-type scale with 1=Slight Stress, 2=Some Stress, 3=Stress, 4=Serious Stress, and 5=Excessive Stress, one activity was rated by respondents as causing close to excessive stress. As shown in Table 8, the item of obtaining program and financial approval (mean 4.02) reflects the activities associated with tracking down additional resources and implies a political behavior to get certain ideas, resolutions, or platforms advanced and approved. The evaluation of faculty was the least stressful activity for governance unit leaders, most likely due to the fact that most governance units do not actively engage in peer evaluation in teaching and research.

Table 8
Skills and Stressors of Faculty Leader Governance Unit Leaders
N=181

Characteristic	Mean	Range	SD
Skills			
Oral communication	4.26	4	.763
Leadership	4.10	4	.792
Organizational ability	4.06	4	.888
Stress tolerance	4.00	4	.676
Decisiveness	3.91	5	.935
Written communication	3.82	5	1.01
Problem analysis	3.80	4	.900
Judgment	3.66	4	.965
Range of interests	3.48	4	.894
Educational values	3.40	5	1.28
Sensitivity	3.39	4	1.16
Stressors			
Obtaining prog/financial approval	4.02	4	.910
Excessively high self expectations	3.90	4	.990
Telephone and visitor interruptions	3.10	4	1.07
Making decisions affecting others	2.80	4	1.01
Job interfering with personal time	2.76	4	1.06
Completing paperwork on time	2.68	4	1.26
Resolving collegial differences	2.64	4	.990
Meetings take too much time	2.51	5	1.16
Having too heavy work load	2.51	4	1.00
Keeping current in discipline	2.50	5	1.22
Preparing manuscripts/presentations	2.25	4	1.09
Complying with institutional rules	2.15	4	1.15
Evaluating faculty performance	1.70	3	.880

Faculty senate presidents and governance unit leaders indicated that to be effective in their jobs, they must have strong, positive oral communication skills, they must be willing to serve as leaders, must have the skills to organize the work of the senate, and must have the patience and tolerance to handle stressful situations. These are the same kinds of skills required of the contemporary college administrator, with the difference being that these college faculty members who step forward to serve in this quasi-administrative post typically have no training and receive no compensation. To develop and foster excellence in the faculty senate presidency, then, there must be a creative search to develop faculty along the lines described here. Additionally, the ambiguity surrounding faculty senates must force administrators and faculty senators to enter into a constructive conversation about the expectations and expected levels of performance of faculty senates and their leaders.

These data findings also indicate that faculty senate presidents do indeed have some agreement on the types of skills necessary to do their job. This provides a strong starting place for faculty development and faculty governance specialists to begin developing training modules to help build stronger faculty governance units. Leadership training can take many forms and be delivered in many different types of packages (workshops, institutes, online or web-based), and the current study provides a good starting point to identify the needed curricular content of these types of training programs. Indeed, with the exception of a pre-conference workshop at the American Association for Higher Education conference, there are few, if any, structured and developed workshops for faculty senate presidents. There is a need to develop this faculty based leadership with the same vigor that administrative techniques are taught in institutes and workshops for college presidents and department chairs, and until the professional community fully embraces the fact that leadership is needed among as well as for faculty, faculty governance units will continue to be wrapped in ambiguity and difficulty in self-definition.

Profile of 2-Year Faculty Governance Leader

Differences in community, junior, and technical college faculty governance leadership could be predicated on any number of variables. Community colleges, for example, with typically local boards of trustees or directors may find more external pressure to conform or respond to community needs or standards, such as to design curriculum for immediate, regional job training. Additionally, many community colleges do not utilize formal differentials for faculty rank and the result might be less internal pressure placed on the social differentiation required for promotion within faculty ranks. In this same regard, faculty may see less of a class-based social structure emerging (full professor versus assistant professor, for example), and the result might be a more open democratic environment.

Gilmour (1991) estimated that 90% of all colleges and universities have some form of faculty governance unit, and the result in the community, junior, and technical college environment would be as many as 1,200 to 1,500 faculty governance bodies in community colleges. This phase of the NDBFIG project randomly selected 300 community, junior, and technical colleges and provided a survey instrument to the leader of the faculty governance unit identified on a web-site. If no leader was identified on the institution's web-site, the instrument was directed to a vice president of academics or dean of instruction with directions to forward it the appropriate person. Data collection took place in 1998-1999, with a total of two follow-up mailings utilized to enhance the overall response rate.

Table 9
Demographic Profile of Community College Governance Unit Leaders
n=244

Characteristic	2-Year FGU
Gender (n=230)	
Female	72 (31%)
Male	158 (69)
Rank (n=209)	
Full Professor	44 (21%)
Associate Prof	19 (9)
Assistant Prof	54 (26)
Other	92 (44)

Table 9 *(continued)*
Demographic Profile of Community College Governance Unit
Leaders

Characteristic	2-Year FGU

Teaching Discipline (n=217)

Liberal Arts	81(37%)
Business	27 (12)
Agriculture	12 (5)
Education	8 (4)
Engineering	6 (3)
Law	0
Medicine	0
Social Work	29 (13)
Communications	11 (5)
Other	43 (20)

Communication Apprehension Levels (n=201)

Written communication (WAT) average score: 64
Oral communication (PRCA) average score: 73

As shown in Table 9, nearly two-thirds of the respondents were male (69%), and held a general faculty rank, termed "other" on the instrument (44%), although 26% did report holding an assistant professorship. This "other" identification was probably the result of many community colleges making use of a general faculty appointment, and not relying on the full-to-assistant professor continuum. Over a third of the respondents (37%) taught in a liberal arts discipline, and a fifth taught in a discipline not identified on the survey, such as fire sciences or protective services. Governance leaders also self-reported a writing apprehension level (mean score) of 64, and an oral communication apprehension level (mean) of 73. This writing apprehension level fell within the standard deviation of the hypothetical mid-point, indicating some apprehension, but not severe enough to impact normal working behaviors.

The 73 mean score on the PRCA also fell within the hypothetical mid-point, and may indicate some situational apprehension.

Tasks and Skills

The community, junior, and technical college governance leaders were also asked about the tasks and skills they face in their roles. They were asked to rate, on a 1-to-5 Likert-type scale their agreement (5=strong agreement, 1=low agreement) that the item was a task they did or if it was a skill they felt they needed. As shown in Table 9, Governance leaders agreed most strongly that the tasks of developing a sense of direction for the unit (mean 4.44) and developing data bases for decision making (mean 4.01) were their most frequent tasks. In a governance unit setting, examples of these tasks might be preparing a vision statement or program of work for the governance body to establish a direction. The development of data sets for governance body decision-making often takes the form of a needs assessments from existing institutional research offices, with little external analysis. Data on such issues as comparable salary incentives or pay increases, budget analyses, and faculty or student behaviors (such as grade distributions or pass/fail ratios) are all examples of data base development for decision making.

Respondents agreed most strongly that the skills needed for effectively leading a faculty governance body are good judgment abilities (mean 4.49), strong oral communication skills (mean 4.19), and good organizational ability (mean 4.10). Sound judgment, as the most agreed upon skill, is perhaps the most difficult to measure and implies something about an individual trait or innate ability of a faculty member to express common sense coupled with belief in a cause. The oral communication skill set is traditionally comprised of abilities in speaking coherently and persuasively and active listening, and is embedded in the intent of the current study's dimensions in communication apprehension. The organizational ability idea is commonly expressed in other areas of administrative performance, and is inclusive of an ability to see and understand a "big" picture for the institution as a whole and beyond a specific organization or group (Westerfield, 1997).

To clarify the ratings of the tasks and skills of community college faculty governance leaders, a factor analysis was conducted on the 15 items that comprised this section of the survey instrument. The exploratory factor analysis is used to identify if variations in data can be "accounted for adequately by a number of basic categories smaller than that with which the investigation was started" (Fruchter, 1954, p. 1). In the analysis, three factors were identified as significant at an alpha level of .5000 or higher. Factor 1, with an overall alpha level of .6832 included: develop a sense of direction (alpha .5346), develop data bases for decision making (.6801), and judgment (.6003). Factor 2, with an overall alpha level of .5844 included: take care of details (.5555), organizational ability (.6325), stress tolerance (.4909), and problem analysis (.5980). Factor 3, with an overall alpha level of .5830, included: develop a sense of pride (.6701) and sensitivity (.4917).

Table 10
Tasks of Community College Faculty Leaders
N=244

Tasks and Skills	Range	SD	Mean
Tasks			
Develop a sense of direction	3	.62	4.44
Develop data bases for decision making	3	.90	4.01
Develop networks and linkages	4	1.00	3.89
Obtain and allocate resources	4	1.00	3.74
Take care of details	3	.93	3.50
Develop a sense of pride	4	.96	3.49
Skills			
Judgement	3	.74	4.49
Oral communication skills	3	.63	4.19
Organizational ability	4	.89	4.10
Written communication skills	4	1.00	4.00
Leadership	3	1.01	4.00
Educational values	3	.99	3.92
Stress tolerance	3	1.00	3.89
Problem analysis	4	1.01	3.74
Sensitivity	4	1.28	3.59

Governance is an important aspect to making community colleges work effectively. The process allows for institutional introspection and reflection, and provides for a creative way to find multiple solutions to complex problems. As structures within structures, they are reliant on the individuals who make them work, particularly the leadership of these organizations –the faculty members who give of their own time and energies to make a difference in the life of the organization.

The process of governance has received a growing amount of attention in the popular and academic press, often in terms of the concept of teamwork, and the current study provides some valuable extensions of this work. First, study findings provide a solid foundation for the additional training of faculty governance leaders. By understanding the stress they encounter and the tasks they face, leadership training can be better tailored to meet specific needs. Second, these findings provide a template for leadership characteristics, and can be criteria for consideration when selecting a faculty governance leader. Governance bodies, for example, might particularly look for faculty who have moderate to low levels of communication apprehension and have a capability to provide direction, have sound judgment, and can effectively broker the political process of obtaining and allocating resources.

As Gilmour has noted, governance is generally a political process that has few certainties. Community colleges, in their efforts to be responsive, need to make strong efforts to better understand and effectively use shared governance bodies. Reliance on senates and councils can be productive, as noted by Armstrong (1999), but more focus needs to be given to how the political aspects of governance leadership can be put into action to improve institutional operations. Future inquiry, by both academics and practitioners, should demonstrate examples of best practice, and how this practice reflects and interprets broad-based, inclusive decision-making at all levels of institutional operation

Motivation

In a separate study of community college faculty leaders, the NDBFIG project surveyed 100 community college faculty governance leaders who were randomly selected from a listing compiled by NDBFIG researchers through the internet and personal contact. Conducted in 1998-1999, the survey was comprised of 14 items which were identified through structured interviews with faculty involved in the governance process at universities participating in the NDBFIG project. Each of the factors was also confirmed as a workplace motivator through an extensive literature review.

Table 11
Community College Faculty Motivation to Assume Leadership Positions
N=84

Factor	Mean	SD	Range	F Prob*
Empowerment	4.58	.593	2	.3023
Sense of responsibility	4.33	.658	2	.4283
Importance of decision-making	4.18	.812	4	.2073
Asked to serve/be involved	4.16	.801	3	.3581
Sense of professionalism	4.01	.752	3	.5217
Sense of ownership	3.91	.871	4	.0170*
Environment of the campus	3.74	1.037	4	.5345
Relationship with administration	3.62	1.058	4	.0630
Communal atmosphere	3.61	1.173	4	.7147
Attitude toward students	3.42	1.026	4	.0941
Quest for knowledge	3.29	1.070	4	.0490*
Self-interest	3.02	1.124	4	.6646

*Denotes significant difference between responses based on task or process orientation.

Of the 14 motivating factors, five had a mean rating of between 4.0 and 5.0, including agreement to strong agreement that the factor was a motivator for the respondent's involvement in faculty governance activities. These five factors included: empowerment (mean 4.58); sense of responsibility (mean 4.33); importance of decision making (mean 4.18); asked to serve/be involved (mean 4.16); and sense of professionalism (mean 4.01; see Table 2). These motivational factors were then stratified by the respondent's classification of role orientation or process orientation to serving as a faculty governance body leader. A one-way Analysis of Variance revealed significant differences on motivational factors: sense of ownership and quest for knowledge (see Table 2 for F Prob). Process-oriented faculty leaders agreed more strongly with both the motivational factors, sense of ownership (process-oriented faculty mean 4.20 compared to 3.72) and quest for knowledge (mean of 3.54 compared to 3.05) as an incentive for involvement, than task-oriented faculty leaders.

The motivation of faculty to be involved with institutional governance has tremendous importance to both administrators and faculty alike, as many institutions are forced to respond to increasingly complex and diverse issues. In the area of distance learning, for example, faculty often volunteer to teach courses utilizing distance education technology, and this type of motivation to try something different in and out of the classroom is vital to future institutional success. The current study, although limited to governance activities, reveals important dimensions for faculty involvement.

First, faculty demonstrated that they are largely involved with institutional governance and decision-making to gain a sense of empowerment, because they feel a sense of professional responsibility, the importance of decision-making, and because they are simply asked to be involved. Responses further demonstrated that faculty desire to be treated with respect and to be given what they may perceive to be real authority and responsibility over decision-making outcomes. This finding was reinforced in the perceptions of an ideal governance structure, where respondents strongly agreed that they should be empowered to question policy.

Second, faculty leaders were found to be only moderately motivated by a quest for knowledge or due to self-interests. This finding represents a sense of altruism among faculty, albeit a cautious one, as noted in the responses to the ideal governance structure which indicated a negative perception of using neutral consultants to resolve conflict.

Interestingly, the orientation of the individual holding the leadership position, whether viewing the voluntary assignment as a task orientation or a process orientation, made a difference in only two of the twelve motivational factors. Thus, the faculty leader may see the facilitating of others' actions similar to the leader who views the role as an instigator of collective faculty action.

Third, findings of the study indicate no clear consensus on validating literature in the area of work motivation. Results of the survey validate, to some extent, Steers and Porter's contention that a combination of variables serve as motivational incentives, yet Farmer's work as well as Maher and Braskmap's appeared to have equal weight in serving as motivational paradigms for college faculty to go beyond their typical workload assignments.

As colleges and universities ask more of their faculty, more study must be incorporated into the realm of adult work motivation as well as lifelong learning to better conceptualize how these faculty members will respond to additional workload assignments. In particular, current events and episodes which voluntarily involve faculty in campus activities may prove to be a fruitful beginning for this much needed research. The current study provides a crucial baseline for this research, yet much must be done, both from faculty and administrative perspectives, to create meaningful mechanisms for motivating the broad spectrum of faculty careers, personalities, and attitudes which create the exciting mosaic of higher education.

Classification of Senate Leaders

A project for the NDBFIG sought to examine the communication patterns of faculty who choose to be involved in a faculty senate or similar organization, and how these patterns played out in the context of senate meetings (Miller, Williams, & Garavalia, forthcoming). By observing an academic year's worth of faculty senate meetings (a total of nine), a team of researcher's coded the communication episodes of faculty. Subsequently drawing on demographic data, the charting communication episodes and passed legislation, motions, and resolutions, findings revealed that specific groups evolved out of similar interests and behaviors. Faculty in these various groups were identified loosely as the "old guard," the "new guard," and "old radicals." The "old guard'" were of former presidents and long time members of the senate. The "new guard" included a number of women, chairs of minimally important senate committees, and generally newer faculty members who had recently been elected to the senate. "Old radicals" were long-time senate members who held the ideal belief that the senate can and should be a powerful force used in general opposition to administration and ever vigilant in defense of faculty rights, discarding any other business as peripheral. Evidence of communication patterns also suggested a fourth, fairly large contingent of newly elected senators who did not control committees, attend meetings somewhat regularly, and were generally quiet and observant yet not involved in senate meetings. The lack of data for the fourth group resulted in its non-inclusion in further discussion of communication patterns.

In an attempt to validate the categories identified, interviews with 12 participating faculty members were undertaken in the 1997-1998 academic year. The interviews included eight males and four females, demographically representing the group of 41 faculty senators. The senators were stratified and selected randomly, with replacement, and asked to participate. Interviews were structured around a set of five pilot-tested questions which asked about senator behaviors and were conducted in teams of two researchers. In addition to behaviors, questions about alliances, power, and organizational effectiveness were asked. Data were recorded manually, but not voice recorded. The data were then considered by the overall research-team (including two faculty and six graduate students) to identify themes in behavior, activity, perceptions, and senate world-view.

Conclusions drawn from the project reinforced much of the exploratory literature identified, suggesting that many senators are involved out of a sense of civic responsibility and love of the institution, while others participated simply because no one else was willing to represent their academic unit. A surprising result of the interviews was the branding of senators and types of senators based on external characteristics and tendencies displayed during senate meetings. The following six categories of leaders were taken from the wording and commentary of the 12 faculty senators:

Rear Guard: These faculty senate leaders see themselves as the appendage to the larger faculty, charged with protecting the body with their own sacrifice. Often serving as a watchdog to campus administration, they operate as a loosely defined or organized collection of faculty who would willingly give up their comfort for the welfare of the campus and the faculty at large.

Politician: Also seen as a "politico," these leaders see themselves as the future leaders of the campus and administration. Deriving their perceived power from the ability to organize and amass the influence of the collective faculty, these leaders find fulfillment in the process of negotiating between administrators and the faculty governance unit. These leaders are primarily concerned with power relationships.

Puppet: These governance leaders find their own hope, aspirations, and enjoyment of the process of shared governance from gaining the approval of campus administration. Drawing largely on the college administration for agenda items, these individuals are reactionary in nature, and often see diplomacy as their trademark characteristic in brokering decisions between the faculty and administration.

Rebel: Also seen as the "vigilante," these concerned faculty members find some enjoyment in the open challenging of administrations, trustees, and even faculty groups which appear compliant to administrative interests. These faculty leaders typically see themselves as the true defenders of faculty interests, and concentrate their efforts on taking pre-emptive actions and challenging administrative actions.

Tactician: Also seen as the faculty governance unit 'mechanic,' these leaders play out their roles as those most concerned about the process rather than the content of decisions. Primarily focusing agenda setting and establishing the tenor, tone, and pace of activity, these individuals often see their role as one of surviving the elected term.

Idealist: These individuals draw tremendous personal fulfillment from the action of being involved and the actual participation in governance activities. These leaders are more likely to be discriminating in selecting issues to challenge and support, have excellent participation records, and feel an obligation to the institution is being served. They see service as "their turn," and comply.

Although most faculty governance unit leaders would typically be an amalgamation of these types, most have a similar characteristic: they did not see themselves as a representative of one group to a larger group. In only rare occasions did the faculty senators who were interviewed rely on town hall meetings or electronic forums to find out how they should vote on key issues or topics, or even know of a fellow senator who used some form of opinion gathering. Faculty governance leaders were seen to be generally expected of some senators, but once elected, they were not fully respected by either the senate or the college's administration.

Impact on Faculty Involvement in Governance

Faculty senators come from a variety of disciplines and they arrive in their respective forums with a broad spectrum of expectations, abilities, and ideas about how to operate their own and the governance unit's business. Based on these differences, it should be no surprise that the individuals they elect to oversee their governance bodies and coordinate their organization's work have a broad spectrum of abilities, vision, insights, and general skills in running a senate. More continual in-depth research into the faculty governance unit leader will prove helpful to further understanding the success or failure of governance bodies, and in understanding the interrelationships of these leaders simultaneously with other faculty members and managers in all levels of administration. The initial NDBFIG project begins an important conversation about who these senators are and what the expectations are for themselves and in their service to others. If shared faculty governance is to survive, then it must be structurally sound and effective in whatever purpose the unit decides upon as central to its existence.

NDBFIG project findings were successful in delineating several important, key elements in understanding the faculty governance unit leader. First, based on data and the type of data collected, a clear boundary of characteristics has been suggested. Although men have typically held a disproportionate percentage of administrative positions, that trend is reversing itself. Mirroring that trend is strength in women holding the governance unit leadership position. This is of course a controversial subject, similar to that of the 11% of the leaders who self-identified themselves as assistant professors, in that a commitment of this nature is typically time consuming and can be politically explosive, so the assistant professor, and perhaps the female faculty member, may end up placing themselves in jeopardy of not being promoted, tenured, or not publishing or conducting an adequate quantity (and quality) of research. As might be expected, the majority of leadership was coming out of associate and full professor ranks, and the liberal arts faculty members seem to drive the units. The preponderance of liberal arts faculty might be because so many general education courses come from the liberal arts, suggesting a political model of electioneering where across-campus name recognition might carry more weight than a discipline-specific representative. The historic nature of the liberal arts faculty members being committed to democracy in education may also provide an incentive for their involvement, perhaps much more so than faculty from engineering or business.

Aside from the specific findings related to skills, tasks, and motivations, the findings also demonstrate that those who are involved at either the two-year or four-year college level do have more in common than might be expected. They have about the same levels of comfort about communication and perceive roughly the same sets of stressors and skills are applicable to the role.

These kinds of findings are also important because they represent an identifiable base to work from for training and development programs. Although institutional histories, memories, and administrators may be widely different, faculty members do have the right and responsibility to ensure their best effort. Often, transitional training programs are inadequate, outdated, and outmoded; faculty governance leaders need a crash course in how college administration works at the detail level (budget, cash flow, priority setting, enrollment management), the often overlooked big picture (how the success of the institution in teaching, research, and service has an impact on the state, nation, constituent), and how to be an effective leader of a disparate, largely autonomous volunteer group of highly trained and specialized individuals. The task is certainly not simple, but does suggest models similar to the Harvard summer institute series and much of the training offered for department chairs by various associations, institutions, and individuals. Another key to emphasize here is the need for multiple people from the senate or governance unit to be trained in these areas; senators, much like college administrators, need to begin thinking about how they will be replaced.

Another central finding that impacts faculty involvement in governance is the inherent lack of community among governance unit participants and among the elected representatives and their constituencies. Senate or governance unit leadership was conveyed to be neither a democracy, nor an administration; somewhat similar to an academic department chair, but more important to the life of faculty rights and institutional integrity. One of the greatest difficulties facing organizations that lack a well-defined community is the notion of transitioning one individual to the next, in this case, a faculty senate president or someone similar who is likely to change every year or every other year. Institutional history and culture and expectations can not be conveyed effectively in a file cabinet, they can not be learned in a day, but they can be shared and learned over time. Does too much time before assuming leadership, however, serve as a disincentive to participation, either for faculty who do not want to wait their turn or for faculty members who get burned-out and feel repressed in the governance body? A number of motivations for involvement were identified, and somewhat in response to Trow's (1990) argument that faculty senators explicitly do not want to go into administration. Trow was probably, however, being extreme and philosophical in this argument. In reality, faculty assume the time-hungry position for a wide number of reasons, specifically including to gain institutional exposure and experience relevant to administrative career building. Important research extending the findings of the motivation for involvement section of this study is needed, and can offer direction, hope, or discouragement related to the future of academic democracy by answering the question of what kind of administrator a former faculty senator becomes. If academic democracies hope to survive and thrive as universities become increasingly corporate-like, the experience of serving in a democratic body has the potential to either make the case for or against continuing and empowering faculty governance units.

Finally, these findings begin to lay the foundation for an expanded framework or categorization of faculty governance unit leaders and more importantly, their units. By offering differences in styles and being able to showcase these catalogs, other governance body leaders may be quicker to respond to the call for creating more accountable and efficient governance units. As noted earlier with the levels of involvement that ranged from manipulation to faculty control, senates and governance bodies can be designed to any number of things, so the success of a governance body leader will be first defining and educating representatives of their task, and then charting a course to help the organization achieve its task or purpose. In a sense, these findings and much of all of the NDBFIG findings seem to stress the need for vision in faculty governance.

Chapter 6

Faculty Involvement in Governance Issues

Dill and Helm (1988) argued that the types of issues that faculty governance units are dealing with have changed substantially. They contend that these units no longer deal with the maintenance of campus life, but rather, that they have fundamentally shifted to strategic policy decisions, basically creating the rules and visions of the institution. Such a broad statement to some extent may reflect a desired thinking, as the literature consistently reports little of what faculty senates and other governance bodies are undertaking. Campus newspapers, alternatively, seem to be favorite reporting places for senate resolutions, debates, and actions, and the *Chronicle of Higher Education* also seems to report the highly visible or radical activities, such as presidential no-confidence votes.

One of the most dramatic changes in recent history has been the emergence of the internet and senate or governance unit-sponsored websites. These websites provide easy access to those interested in governance unit activities, and allow for an easy cataloging of the unit's history. As webpages change frequently, there is not much use reporting a listing of websites here, but a simple internet search or review of a college or university's website will commonly reveal names of faculty representatives, contact information, meeting agendas and minutes, passed policies, constitutions, by-laws, and even budget information.

There is a great value in knowing and better understanding what faculty governance units are involved with and the kinds of things they talk about, debate, and vote on. Although the literature base is sporadic at best, there are allusions to a common understanding about what senates and other bodies undertake. Are they as restricted as Miles (1997A) suggested in what they can undertake? Or do their votes and actions make a substantial difference in how the institution operates? This current chapter was designed to look at what governance units are talking about and what kinds of issues they address, rather than the impact of those decisions. Indeed, the impact of senate behaviors and the legality and binding nature of those decisions is an important point for further research. Additionally, a comprehensive cataloging of faculty governance units, including senates and staff councils, would be meaningful in shaping and understanding how policy is formed and implemented.

The NDBFIG project allowed for the national observation of what faculty governance bodies were undertaking, including the kinds of topics they discussed that were reported, a survey of faculty governance leaders, and two case studies of the topics faculty governance unit considered.

National Observation

One of the clearest avenues for identifying the kinds of issues faculty are involved with in decision-making in formal governance units is how these items are reported by neutral parties. The Chronicle of Higher Education, a weekly newspaper devoted to the higher education industry, is perhaps the only and certainly most comprehensive source for information on what is happening inside higher education institutions. The Chronicle, a newspaper style publication, typically includes news sections on technology, students, athletics, research, finance, and faculty. Other mechanisms certainly exist for looking at particular segments of higher education as an industry, such as *U Business* and *Educause*, although they would be unlikely sources for information about faculty governance units. By examining reported trends, a status report on the state of faculty involvement in governance can be developed and utilized as a point for meaningful change or institutional growth in terms of shared authority.

Data in this portion of NDBFIG research were collected by reviewing four years of *The Chronicle of Higher Education*, beginning August 10, 1994 and ending November 21, 1997. Each issue was studied to identify any article or news event description related to faculty involvement in governance. Broadly, these topics included faculty support for administrative bodies, faculty strikes, faculty involvement in workload disagreements, planning, and support, or lack thereof, for administrative decision-making. A total of 26 articles from 132 issues of *The Chronicle* were identified for use in data analysis.

1994

Faculty strikes or walk-outs were frequent occurrences in 1994. Although the American Association for University Professors (AAUP) claimed that faculty strikes are rare, there were at least four faculty strikes in 1994. In August, the demoralized faculty at the University of New Hampshire threatened to strike because of low faculty pay. The following month, the faculty voted 226 to 58 to strike. Around the same time, faculty members at Wayne State University and Oakland University held strikes or walk-outs over salary and benefit issues. Although the faculty at the University of New Hampshire accepted a two-year contract, ultimately avoiding the strike, the Wayne State faculty were on strike for two days. In October, the faculty at the C. W. Post campus of Long Island University voted to strike, complaining of heavy courseloads. After three days, the faculty returned to their classrooms without reaching agreement or acquiring a new contract.

Another frequent issue during the year was faculty members' perceptions of overbearing administrators. In late September, the faculty of the University of Colorado at Boulder argued that the Board of Trustees violated a perceived fundamental standard of faculty governance by promoting a non-supported faculty member. The faculty collectively asserted that this act was a clear violation of their academic freedom.

In November, the faculty at York College of the City University of New York issued a no confidence vote of 94 to 25 for their president. The vote came shortly after it was announced that CUNY auditors were investigating the president's inappropriate use of a discretionary fund. Although the president believed that faculty members were too hasty in passing judgment, faculty union members encouraged the university to take quick action and replace the president. In December, faculty at Rutgers University in New Jersey argued that the administration was too 'heavy handed.' They believed that speaking out against administrators resulted in office reassignments, with the goal of isolating 'trouble makers.'

And in the summer of 1994, faculty members at Bennington College argued that the administration's restructuring plan destroyed faculty structures of governance. The new restructuring plan called for the dismissal of 26 faculty members.

1995

In January, a federal review panel, the Commission on the Future of Worker-Management Relations, encouraged Congress to rewrite the definition of managerial employees. The Commission argued that the new definition should allow faculty members a greater role in decision-making without the fear of being "stripped" of their collective bargaining rights.

The unifying theme for the year was the distrust of faculty of overpower or overbearing administrators. In January, faculty members at Clemson University complained that the new restructuring plan gave more power to administrators over decisions regarding tenure and money appropriation. Leaders of the faculty senate claimed that the new plan removed faculty members from the decision-making process. In March, faculty members at James Madison University voted no confidence in their president by a vote of 305 to 197. They alleged that the new restructuring plan cut faculty members from governance procedures and afforded too much power to administrators. A few months later, an organized faculty group called the Faculty for Responsible Change sued the university for attempting to remove faculty from decision-making.

In September, 110 faculty members at Rutgers expressed their "deep discontent" in their president. They argued that the president rarely consulted with faculty members on academic matters. And in December, 65 faculty members at Florida A&M University filed grievances against the university, alleging a violation of their union contract. Faculty members claimed that their workload was not similar to those in other state university system institutions.

1996

Faculty again expressed their belief that they were restricted or shut out of the decision making process throughout 1996. In February, faculty members in the University of California System argued that the University Regents were preventing them from making key decisions regarding bans on racial preferences. Four months later, the AAUP condemned the Regents for acting alone. The AAUP argued that by acting alone, the regents violated the basic principle of shared governance. In April, the Academic Senate of Wayne State University voted no confidence in the new policies created by its president by a vote of 38 to 11. After speaking to various department heads, the president agreed to make minor changes to the new policies. However, his decision not to change some of the new policies angered faculty members, who protested that the policies were a violation of their academic freedom. In the same month, faculty members at Francis Marion University voted no confidence in their president. They claimed that he made decisions regarding curriculum and tenure, without seeking advice from the faculty senate or faculty members in general.

In May, the faculty at Goddard College voted no confidence in their president by a vote of 42 to 1. Faculty members argued that the president gave no regard to the tradition of shared governance on campus by making unilateral decisions regarding curriculum and faculty hiring. In July, members of the faculty union at the University of the District of Columbia sued the university for barring union officers from serving in the university senate. Union members alleged that their constitutional rights to freedom of association had been violated.

In September, angered faculty members at the University of Minnesota protested new policy proposals. They claimed that the new policies would eliminate tenure and give too much power to administrators. And in December, faculty members at the University of Notre Dame voted 29 to 5 their 'strong disapproval' of the president's involvement in a faculty hiring decision. In that instance, faculty and the department chair of the theology department gave negative recommendations regarding a candidate for a professorship, yet the president offered the candidate the position. Faculty members reported that the president's decision was a violation of the trust that they believed should exist between faculty and administrators.

1997

Again, the most pressing issue of the year was the power and influence of administrators. In May, the Board of Trustees at Francis Marion University dismantled the faculty senate after the senate failed to implement a plan devised by the Board. Faculty members argued that the action of the Trustees destroyed all structures of shared governance, and many believed that the Board's decision was in reaction to the faculty's vote of no confidence.

In June, faculty members at Santa Rosa Junior College voted no confidence in their president. Faculty were upset when they discovered that the president ordered searches of their faculty offices, personnel files, and computers. They argued that the president violated their trust and constitutional rights to privacy.

In October, faculty members at the University of Michigan at Dearborn objected to a new policy on tenure and promotion. They claimed that the new policy gave too much power to administrators, and allowed some faculty members to receive tenure although other faculty members had recommended otherwise. In the next month, faculty members at Wayne State University argued that the administration attempted to take away their rights to privacy when the president issued his new policy on the use of university computer systems. In his policy, the president indicated that the university had the authority to monitor e-mail and internet access, and he mandated that university computers were to be strictly used for university related business. Faculty members claimed that the president was taking a "tyrannical approach" to governance.

Overall

Disagreements over role responsibilities often lead to increased animosity between those making the decisions. While faculty and administrators alike struggle to define their position in shared governance systems, the institutional decision-making process often suffers. Findings of the research indicate that faculty are most often dissatisfied with issues involving the appropriation of power. Between 1994 and 1997, eight cases of faculties voting no confidence were observed, and of these eight cases, seven were in direct response to administrative policies or procedures that were viewed as attempts to undermine the trust of the faculty or the governance system of the individual institution. In addition, two faculty unions filed class actions suits against their respective institutions over rights to participate in decision-making. Restructuring plans that afforded too much power to administrators also produced heated debates among faculty and administrators during this time.

Shared authority in higher education, as alluded to in the current events, has become increasingly political and legal in nature. This politicization has benefits for faculty serving as a watch-dog to administrative behaviors, but has serious shortcomings in regard to efficiency and effectiveness.

Leaders Respond

As argued in the previous chapter, governance unit leaders often set the agenda of issues to be addressed by their governance body. Assuming the leaders have a somewhat active direction and can convey the topics that will be considered and the amount of governance time committed to these topics. This can be true from any number of perspectives, including administrative desires for units to deal with particular issues, prior year unit unfinished business and carry over items, and the need of the corporate- university to invest in planning. Some faculty governance units have also reported taking the time to develop strategic and long-range plans, and the result is the acceptance of the assumption that governance unit leaders can indeed predict to a large extent what important topics their body will consider. Additionally, as many governance unit leaders have year-around access to administrative meetings and conduct their own executive council or committee business during summer months, it should be increasingly possible for these governance units to have expectations for the types of issues (curriculum versus management, for example) that will be placed on the unit's agenda.

To develop a better understanding of the important topics addressed by faculty governance bodies, a national panel of governance unit leaders were asked to respond to the open ended question: What important topics will your faculty governance unit deal with during the next academic year? A total of 50 randomly selected faculty senate presidents at four-year land grant and state universities were selected to participate in the study, and just over half (n=28; 56%) responded. Participants were provided up to five lines to answer the question, although they were instructed that they could use additional paper if necessary. This component of the research was intended to be entirely exploratory to help identify topics for further research. Surveys were mailed to governance unit leaders in August 2000, with the assumption that as they built their agendas or programs of work for the coming year they would have a sense of the kinds of things they would be dealing with. One follow-up mailing was conducted with no additional surveys being returned.

As shown in Table 12, the most often cited issue to be addressed was that of tenure (n=14; 50% of respondents). This was not considered surprising considering the popular attention tenure has received in recent years, namely, conversations about replacing tenure with term contracts or eliminating any vestige of tenure altogether. The use of part-time faculty and institutional funding were the second most frequently cited issues to be addressed by governance units, each being named by eight governance unit leaders (28% of the respondents). A similar percentage of respondents identified the demise of the university as it becomes corporatized and technology issues were both named by seven respondents (25%). So although the primary claim to faculty governance unit empowerment is curricular based, no exclusive curriculum issues were identified prior to the start of their unit's sessions. Tenure and the use of part-time faculty can be argued under the nomenclature of curriculum and both have had a good deal of recent discussion and debate, yet both could also be argued to be personnel and budget policies. Technology as an agenda item was vague so that there could be no clear delineation of whether this was a business issue or curriculum issue. Technology in teaching was identified by one other respondent, yet the wording of this item suggests something much more specific than simply "technology" or "technology issues," and has ramifications for such areas as distance and distributed learning, on-line course instruction, web-page hosting and support, integration into teaching, support for faculty training, etc. Similarly, institutional funding and resources could be argued as either an institutional business operation, which many faculty might feel to be inappropriate for an academic senate, for example, or considered as a variable impacting academic affairs.

Two relatively self-referential items were named by six governance leaders (21% of respondents), including maintaining faculty power and addressing the issue of whether or not faculty senates are "worth it." These are clearly internal questions that have external impacts, including the governance body's relationship with constituents, administrators, students, and boards. An additional item identified by one respondent was the erosion of academic freedom, and another respondent identified faculty senate efficiency. Both of these could be added to the other two to suggest the even more acute issue of self-diagnosis (what is the state of the faculty governance unit?) or self-reflection, certainly an issue worthy of organizational growth and a necessity for organizational behavior.

Other items were classified into two broad categories: structure and core values/mission. The items under the classification of structure dealt primarily with how the governance unit would operate. Apathy and involvement was identified most frequently along with time to accomplish work/workload (both n=5; 18%). These items certainly conveyed a sense of various institutional cultures by identifying issues to be dealt with such as combativeness with administration, tension between quality and efficiency, and asking about responsibility for teaching. The core values/mission category had distance education as the most frequently cited issue (n=4; 14%) followed by the engagement of the university with society (n=2; 7%). Many of these eight items were vague and could be interpreted in multiple ways. Relevance and credibility, for instance, could be related to curriculum and external views of the institution, or could be viewed in relationship to the success and working of the faculty governance unit.

Overall the responses provided a good first step into looking at how faculty governance units build their agendas and the kinds of things they talk and think about in relation to the business of their senates and forums. The more specific, and anticipated, responses pertaining to campus-based issues were not identified by respondents, which could mean that either the governance unit leaders did not know what they will be dealing with in the coming months, that the question needed refinement, or that faculty governance units really do spend a good deal of time talking about what they are supposed to be doing and how they are supposed to be doing it. Future researchers in this area might find it helpful to catalog a variety of topics and ask governance unit leaders to respond to their likeliness that they will be dealing with the issue.

Table 12
Topics Addressed by Faculty Senates in 2000-2001

Topic	Frequency Cited
Tenure	14
Part-time faculty use	8
Institutional funding/resources	8
Demise of the university as it becomes corporatized in favor of efficiency	7
Technology	7
Maintaining faculty power to make decisions in light of the emerging corporate model	6
Are faculty senates worth it?	6
Faculty unions/unity	4
Faculty merit rewards	3
Protection of curriculum	3
Erosion of academic freedom	2
Conduct research	1
Interdisciplinary issues	1

Table 12 *(continued)*
Topics Addressed by Faculty Senates in 2000-2001

Topic	Frequency Cited
Technology and teaching	1
Faculty senate efficiency	1
Institutional autonomy	1
Public perception of faculty work	1
Faculty turnover	1

Structure

Apathy and involvement	5
Time to accomplish work/workload	5
Faculty development	3
Identification of institutional	3
Student quality/issues	3
Combativeness of administration	3
Legislative issues	2
Tension between quality and efficiency	2
Who is taking care of teaching	1

Core Values/Mission

Distance education	4
Engagement of the university with society	2
Relevance	1
Credibility	1
Impact	1
Communication	1
Role	1
Academic freedom	1

Case 1: A Community College

In 1998, data from an urban community college in Birmingham, Alabama was reviewed to identify the specific issues dealt with by one institution. The community college, founded in 1963 as part of the state's response to demand for higher education, enrolled approximately 4,000 full-time equivalent students and employed 100 full-time and 250 part-time teaching faculty. From the full-time teaching faculty, a Faculty Senate (FS) was elected annually. Within this council a Faculty Senate Council (FSC) of, on average, 17 members was elected bi-annually from within its own ranks. The FSC served as a coordinating body for the FS, and held responsibility for arranging meetings, distributing minutes and agendas, and implementing FS policy.

For the case study, all minutes and meeting records from 1987-1997 were collected, chronologically organized, and reviewed. The range of issues varied based on the year and on the composition of both the FS and the FSC. Meeting minutes were determined to be troublesome in delineating what was an actual item on the agenda, what issues came out of casual conversation, and what topics were entirely extraneous to the operation and business of the FS and FSC (such as personal health, office related personal conversation, personal interactions with students and fellow faculty, etc.). Subsequently, the decision was made to look exclusively at the motions made in both organizations. As a note to Table 13, both groups operated somewhat independently, and motions presented in one body did not necessarily come to a vote in the other body.

The academic years involved in the study were 1987-1988 through 1997-1998, for a total of 11 academic years. During that time, the FSC considered 26 motions, all of which received passing votes. In three of those years, however, no motions were presented and voted on by the FSC. Many of the topics they considered were academic-related (such as considering the quarter to semester transition, examining advising procedures, grading policies), but an equal number were representative of the business of the institution (recycling, structure of the media center, administrative pay, disclosure of institutional investment information, campus security, no smoking policy, etc.). The most dominant theme of issues considered could be that of administrative and faculty trust, as defined by eight different motions that dealt with how the FSC and the administration operate. An example of this kind of thinking was the motion to freeze administrative pay and to disclose budget, salary, and investment information. This thinking can often be representative of one group (the faculty) who question how resources are being allocated (by administrators) and who have concern over the legitimacy of those distributions. The second theme was clearly that of academic-business affairs, that is, how grades are awarded, what the structure of classes can and should look like, workload equity, and the honor council. Generally, then, the FSC had a balance between the traditional areas of curricular and academic management and broader institutional operations questions.

The Faculty Senate was slightly more active in the motions they presented, averaging nearly three per year for a total of 30. In the 1996 academic year, the FS presented and voted on no motions. Of the 30 that were presented, seven were either tabled or did not receive a passing vote. The FS considered fewer institutional, business-related motions than their FSC counterparts (they did consider a motion from an AIDS task force, studied campus safety, considered a motion on business restructuring for the college, and awarded several scholarships). The FSC mirrored many of the topics voted on by the FSC (such as advising, workload, differentiating between full- and part-time faculty members, and salary raise information), and also issued several commendations for commitment to the institution to individuals such as the college's president. The FSC did, however, spend a great deal more time considering the role of faculty in governance, supporting motions on faculty rights, and revising the FS constitution. The FS also considered the importance of faculty professional development and the college's merger with another campus in the community, although both motions ultimately failed.

The FS largely worked within the boundaries of traditional faculty governance units by dealing with issues related to curriculum and academic affairs. The lines between academic affairs and business operations, however, can be difficult to differentiate, as issues such as faculty workload, faculty pay, student advising, and campus calendar can all permeate both the worlds of academic affairs and business operations. The FS also seemed to undertake a more symbolic role in recognizing individuals who had an impact on the campus, providing a commendation to the college's president and awarding faculty senate scholarships. Both of these actions may not directly impact the academic nature of the institution, but do reflect a traditional role of faculty in serving as the protectorate of institutional integrity.

The Jefferson State Community College case study provides an excellent example of the difficulties associated with shared governance. From one perspective they are entirely within their historically-defined rights to debate and offer recommendations on issues impacting curriculum and curricular delivery. Other topics are clearly outside of the academic realm but are consistent with the mission of advancing the institution. An interesting follow-up study to a case study of this nature would have been the extent to which the passed motions were implemented as policy. Did, for example, the Faculty Senate's suggestion for a definition of full-time faculty actually take effect? Can the Faculty Senate or Senate Council prescribe what a standard teaching workload should be? Do both bodies have any legitimate power to endorse a college's merger? All are logical extensions of the exploration of topics and desperately need attention. Although there has been reference to faculty governance units serving as enablers to big decisions on campus, the 'little' decisions that appear to be substantial on a monthly basis are the ones that need to be considered, with the role of the senate defined, refined, and agreed upon by all parties involved.

Table 13

Motions Considered by the Jefferson State Community College Faculty Senate and Faculty Senate Council between 1987 and 1997

Year		Issue or topic of motion
1987	FSC	Campus security and safety Legislative support
	FS	Faculty senate scholarships Outstanding faculty member qualifications Faculty/student advising Campus security and safety questionnaire AIDS Committee task force*
1988	FSC	No motions
	FS	Outstanding faculty member Quarter/semester conversion issue Faculty Senate scholarships Definition of full-time faculty Definition of full-time faculty (amendment)* Create the position "instructor emeritus"
1989	FSC	Update name of institution Academic honesty committee Full-time/part-time faculty ratios Campus no smoking policy Instructor emeritus criteria
	FS	Commendation to college president Revision of Faculty Senate constitution**
1990	FSC	Surveying advising procedures Invite State Board of Education to address faculty Address college advising procedures To oppose the F/A grading policy change Concerns about the South Campus Faculty/staff salary information publicized Validity of credit hour production

Table 13 *(continued)*
Motions Considered by the Jefferson State Community College Faculty Senate and Faculty Senate Council between 1987 and 1997

Year		*Issue or topic of motion*
	FS	Faculty/Staff salary information publicized
		Faculty/Staff salary information survey*
		Validity of credit hour production

Motions Considered 1987 and 1997

Year		*Issue or topic of motion*
1991	FSC	Recycling on campus
		Faculty input into administrative decision-making
		To oppose faculty teaching load revision
		All salary information be public
	FS	Praise a retiring administrator
		To oppose an increased faculty teaching load
		Increase faculty input to decision-making
1992	FSC	No motions presented
	FS	Faculty Senate scholarships
		Faculty rights resolution
		To table the faculty rights resolution*
		Advising and registration procedures
1993	FSC	Allow Faculty Senate president access to Academic Administration Council
		Media Center independence
		Freeze on administrative pay raises and promotions
		Support the president's pursuit of equity funding
	FS	Campus business operations revision*
		Inclusion of materials in Faculty Senate minutes

Table 13 (*continued*)
Motions Considered 1987 and 1997

Year		Issue or topic of motion
1994	FSC	Allow an academic division use of instructor emeritus facilities
	FS	Faculty Senate Constitution revision College merger* Consistency in salary raise procedures
1995	FSC	Requesting administrative staff to present budget to faculty
	FS	Faculty rights resolution*
1996	FSC	No motions presented
	FS	No motions presented
1997	FSC	Distribute financial investment information to all faculty
	FS	Make professional development a top priority*

*Motion did not pass, was tabled or not recorded.
**Motion passed unanimously.

Case 2: An Academic College

The faculty forum at this case study college in a public, doctoral-intensive research-university, was designed in 1993 to facilitate the involvement of faculty in the College. The forum was designed primarily around the concepts of larger academic senates, including a slate of officers and seven committees, referred to as "action teams" to handle specific items of business and to conduct further research and study specific issues of concern. Action teams were designed around topical rather than functional areas, and included: finance and facilities, curriculum, external services and technology, faculty affairs, student affairs, research, and governance and operations.

Although the university involved in the research was classified as a Carnegie doctoral granting (intensive) institution, recent movements had been made in the reward and tenure structure to reclassify the institution as primarily a research-university (Carnegie 2000 extensive). These movements largely dealt with rewarding grant writing and increasing the expectation of publications to earn tenure and receive continuous appointment as a graduate faculty member.

By design, the first three Thursday afternoons of the month were reserved for forum activities. The first Thursday was reserved for action team meetings, the second for the forum's executive council meeting, and the third for all-faculty meetings. Additional meetings, such as those with the Dean of the College, were scheduled on an as-needed basis. The current study was concerned only with the all-faculty meetings.

The College was divided into two broad departments or schools. Each included programs, typically with individual program chairs coordinating each division that might be considered an academic "department" at other institutions. These program chairs had individually arranged work assignments, often receiving one-quarter release time from teaching and research to serve as a program chair.

The schools, Teacher Education and Professional Studies, were coordinated by school heads, who were considered faculty rather than administrators, being given half-time release for administrative duties. Teacher Education contained seven individual academic programs all related to teacher certification opportunities, although several degree options included non-teacher certification programs. The Professional Studies school contained six individual academic programs, primarily including graduate programs and several undergraduate programs which had teaching and non-teaching certification opportunities.

The College had an undergraduate full-time student equivalent enrollment of approximately 1,700 students and 700 graduate students. Both of these enrollment figures reflected increases over the past decade, rising from 1,067 undergraduates and 572 graduate students in 1985. Faculty in the College had declined from 90 tenure-earning positions in the 1991 academic year to 77 tenure-earning positions in the 1995 academic year.

An additional item of note was the change in the College's leadership. A new dean was hired from another institution during the summer prior to the year of study. The new dean was appointed with tenure in Professional Studies school, and during the course of the year of study several personnel changes in the College's administration were made.

Attendance Patterns

For the entire college, Full-Professors (n=37) attended meetings 43% of the time, Associate Professors (n=7) attended meetings 65% of the time, and Assistant Professors (n=27) attended meetings 53% of the time (see Table 14). Of the faculty in Teacher Education, Full-Professors (n=20) attended meetings 48% of the time, Associate Professors (n-6) attended 62% of the meetings, and Assistant Professors (n=15) attended 51% of the meetings. In Professional Studies, Full-Professors (n=17) attended 37% of the meetings, the Associate Professor (n=1) attended 87% of the meetings, and Assistant Professors (n=12) attended 55% of the meetings (see Table 18).

Faculty holding administrative positions in the Dean's Office, all classified as Full-Professors, attended 31% of the meetings. Table 14. Attendance Patterns by Rank and Tenure Status

Table 14
Attendance Patterns by Rank and Tenure Status

Faculty Forum Meeting Attendance

Case#	Rank	Tenure	1	2	3	4	5	6	7	8	% Att
School of Teacher Education											
1	3	N									0
2	3	N		X	X		X		X	X	62
3	1	Y	X	X	X		X	X	X	X	87
4	1	Y	X	X	X			X			50
5	1	Y		X		X					25
6	1	Y	X	X	X	X	X	X	X	X	100
7	3	N	X	X		X	X	X			62
8	3	N					X	X			25
9	3	N	X	X						X	37
10	3	N	X	X				X			37
11	3	N				X			X		25
12	1	Y									0
13	1	Y	X		X	X	X	X	X	X	87
14	3	N	X		X	X	X	X	X	X	87
15	3	N	X	X	X			X		X	62
16	3	N				X	X				25
17	2	Y	X	X			X		X		50
18	1	Y					X				12
19	1	Y			X	X					25
20	2	Y		X		X			X		37
21	1	Y				X	X				25
22	1	Y	X		X		X		X		50
23	2	Y	X				X	X	X		50
24	3	N		X	X	X	X			X	62
25	3	N	X	X			X	X			50
26	1	Y	X	X	X		X	X	X		75
27	2	Y									0
28	3	N		X	X	X	X	X	X		75
29	2	Y	X	X			X	X	X		X	75
30	3	N	X	X			X	X	X	X		75

Table 14 *(continued)*
Attendance Patterns by Rank and Tenure Status

						Faculty Forum Meeting Attendance					
Case#	*Rank*	*Tenure*	*1*	*2*	*3*	*4*	*5*	*6*	*7*	*8*	*% Att*
School of											
Teacher Education											
31	2	N	X		X	X	X	X	X		87
32	1	Y	X	X	X	X	X	X	X	X	100
33	1	N	X	X		X		X	X		62
34	1	Y	X	X	X	X	X	X		X	87
35	1	Y	X		X	X					37
36	1	Y	X								12
37	1	Y		X	X						25
38	1	Y	X								12
39	1	Y		X							12
40	3	N	X	X		X	X	X	X	X	87
41	1	Y	X	X	X	X	X		X	X	87
	SUBTOTAL		25	26	18	20	24	20	18	13	50%
School of											
Professional Studies											
42	3	N	X	X	X		X		X	X	75
43	1	Y									0
44	3	N	X		X						25
45	1	Y	X						X		25
46	1	Y							X		12
47	1	Y			X		X		X		37
48	3	N	X	X		X	X		X		62
49	3	N	X	X	X	X	X	X	X	X	100
50	1	N	X	X		X	X	X	X	X	87
51	1	Y				X	X		X		37
52	1	Y	X	X		X	X	X	X	X	87
53	3	N		X	X	X	X	X	X	X	87
54	2	N	X	X	X	X	X	X		X	87

Table 14 *(continued)*
Attendance Patterns by Rank and Tenure Status

			Faculty Forum Meeting Attendance								
Case #	*Rank*	*Tenure*	*1*	*2*	*3*	*4*	*5*	*6*	*7*	*8*	*%Att*
School of											
Professional Studies											
55	1	Y		X		X					25
56	3	N	X		X	X	X	X	X	X	87
57	3	N	X	X							25
58	1	Y	X	X						25	25
59	1	Y									0
60	3	N	X		X		X	X		50	50
61	3	N									0
62	1	Y	X				X	X		X	50
63	1	Y	X	X	X	X	X	X	X	X	100
64	1	Y									0
65	3	N	X	X			X			X	50
66	3	N	X	X	X	X	X	X		X	87
67	1	Y	X	X	X	X	X	X	X	X	100
SUBTOTAL			15	15	11	13	15	10	14	13	53%
TOTAL:			40	41	29	33	39	30	32	26	51%

Agendas

Agendas for each meeting were scheduled to be distributed on the Monday preceding each faculty forum meeting (see Figure 5 for sample agenda). Items for the agenda were approved by the chairs of each Action Team along with four elected Forum "directors," all of whom comprised the forum's executive "Faculty Council." The Council met once per month to address issues to be included on the forum agenda as well as to examine motions and refer new business to appropriate Action Teams.

Agendas typically varied in content from meeting to meeting, but generally followed a similar pattern, including Action Team reports, reports from other faculty representatives to College and University committees, and included motions for faculty vote under new business. Issues related to institutional research necessary for motion advancement were considered at the Action Team level, and were sent to Forum members via a standardized format for making motions.

Figure 5
Sample Forum Meeting Agenda
Faculty Forum Agenda
Room 100, Main Hall, 3:30 PM

---

1. Call to Order
2. Reading and Approval of Minutes
3. Reports from Officers and Action Teams
   a. Officers
   b. Action Teams
      i.   Finances and Facilities
      ii. Curriculum
      iii. External Services and Technology
      iv. Faculty Affairs
      v.   Governance and Operations
      vi. Research
      vii. Student Affairs
4. Reports from College Wide Committees
5. Reports from Faculty Senators, Graduate Council Members
6. Reports from Members of the University Committees
7. New Business
8. Announcements (such as memorial reception/fund contributions, faculty identification cards, library changes, etc.)
9. Adjournment

Decisions

A total of 39 motions were presented for action to the faculty forum during the 1995-1996 academic year. Of these motions, 36 (92%) were passed, 3 failed, and 1 was tabled with no further action. The majority of the motions were made by untenured faculty (n=26; 66%), as compared to tenured faculty (n=13; 33%) and 69% of all motions passed were made by untenured faculty. Conversely, two of the three motions which failed were made by tenured faculty. The motions included in the analysis excluded all those relating to the approval of meeting minutes and for adjournment.

Of the motions passed, 55% (n=20) related to the business operations of running the faculty governance unit. These included such items as committee appointments, methods for reporting information to the faculty forum, officer elections, and the governance of the Forum. Additionally, five of the passed motions (14%) related to procedural issues in the forum, such as calling the question to vote and referring motions to committees (Action Team). Of the remaining passed motions, eight dealt with college-wide operations, and one related to an amendment to the college-wide operations motion. Two of the motions which were not passed dealt with college-wide operations, and the third motion which did not pass was an amendment to an earlier motion of college operations.

Issues Considered

A variety of issues were dealt with at various Action Team levels and never surfaced during forum meetings. Four issues, however, were brought to the attention of the forum and all eventually required a vote. These issues included: methods for determining merit pay and who should be involved with what criteria; curriculum requirements, specifically relating to undergraduate entrance grade point averages; the College's mission statement, consistent with accreditation concerns; and the procedure for students in the College for filing a grievance.

Discussion

The faculty governance unit described here represents a unique addition to institutionally focused and directed faculty senates and councils. As institutional decision-making is increasingly directed at academic unit responsibilities, such as the movement toward responsibility centered budgeting, collective Faculty measures such as the faculty forum may grow even more popular.

The faculty forum introduced several measures particularly sensitive in the current higher education debate. Issues such as merit pay, college entrance, the role and mission of academic units, and student centered procedures have all arisen to the forefront of higher education discussions in recent years. In particular, the current trend of increased litigation seems to be a motivating factor for the forum to debate and decide on filing academic as well as non-academic grievances and appeals of these grievances, providing an area of contemplation for both procedural and substantive due process by college administrators. Additionally, the definition of the college through role and mission statement wording reflects current trends in professional schools to provide a statement of preparing scholars and practitioners. Similarly, such action reflects positive self-study concerning what is currently being done and what can be done in the future.

Attendance and voting patterns provided no generalizable data to reinforce some perceptions that older, more secure faculty provide the dynamic leadership of rebellion. Conversely, the forum case indicates that faculty at all levels are moderately involved, and few appeared to provide the inspiration or leadership necessary to rally all faculty to participate. These attendance patterns also seem to reflect a concept of "watch-dog" faculty representation, where a few highly dedicated faculty members constantly evaluate and provide feedback on college wide and institutional decisions. This mentality provides a means of disproportionate workload, but does potentially provide a mechanism for altering faculty to issues which may inspire or motivate them to become involved.

Similar to the decision-making and voting procedures, the agendas developed for the forum appeared consistent with tradition, and seemed to provide an outlet for faculty debate, if necessary. The emphasis on action team and committee reports demonstrated the need to somehow effectively communicate important information to all faculty. Despite the ingenuity of providing reports, attendance behaviors appeared to have a somewhat nullifying effect on information dissemination.

Overall, the forum provided the impression of a means to articulate faculty needs and desires, but perhaps most importantly, serves as a mechanism for faculty to vent frustrations and concerns related to college-wide decision-making and policy. Consider the modest participation, the forum did provide a valuable outlet for faculty voices to be heard. Whether or not the voices will be heeded provides a unique and rich area for further dialogue and research, one which must be examined both from the perspective of participating and non-participating faculty as well as a host of administrators.

Impact on Faculty Involvement in Governance

Faculty governance units have many different looks and consider many different kinds of issues, ranging from the somewhat radical to the mundane operations of university life. The examples explored here offer a glimpse into what is currently happening, and offer the important suggestion that there needs to be considerably more work done on governance units as complex organizations. Some form of cataloging or classification of faculty senates would be a helpful first step, and might include variations arranged along the lines of the ladder of faculty governance discussed earlier. In such a scenario, there might be a Presentation Unit that focuses more on the presentation of information (non-participation in college decision-making) rather than decision-making. Collaborative Units might be those that actually make decisions that are implemented and have various forms of power, representing the opposite end of a spectrum with Presentation units. A middle category might be Emerging Governance Units, representing those bodies that serve a valuable resource in allowing faculty to speak out on important issues, but might not have the authority or respectability to make binding institutional decisions.

The important issue to draw from even a rudimentary classification such as a Presentation-Emerging-Collaborative model is that different kinds of governance units consider different kinds of issues. The topics identified here clearly spell out that governance bodies are active at the very least within themselves and in their search to define who they are and the kinds of things they represent. The difficulty, though, is that senates and governance units are not supposed to be about themselves; they are supposed to be about the faculty, the curriculum, the intellectual life of an institution and all that the institution can and should be. The literature, particularly Aronowitz (2000), seem to recognize that faculty members do indeed represent the best and worst of higher education. They are the intellectual pillars on which higher education is built, and as colleges and universities grow in mirroring corporate structures, the importance placed on academic integrity is challenged, although often not overtly, and faculty are forced to be reactionary. And while faculty governance units can be put under a microscope for their reactionary behaviors (no confidence votes, etc.), the same is seldom true for administrators who attempt to define their own visions without consultation.

The topics addressed by governance units certainly reinforce the conception that these bodies often do not have a clear picture of what they are supposed to do, and that in all probability the traditions of one leadership team to the next form the foundation of what will be done and how it will get accomplished. This mentality, while entirely appropriate for a volunteer association framed loosely around 'academic affairs,' leaves room for a great deal of negotiation of topics, timelines, and methods. One key difficulty, though, is that the generation of faculty members who found empowerment in formal governance units as defenders of academic freedoms have not trained their successors well, and in fact, by belaboring certain personal or long-standing issues, can serve as a disincentive for the most qualified and respected members of the academic community to become disengaged and not involved.

The somewhat clear direction for governance units, then, is to focus attention on the behaviors of the organization, to offer purposeful and important actions that engage those around them, and to work hard to ensure that they respond to constituent needs. At the same time, though, they must continually guard the core integrity that has traditionally been the stronghold of the American university. Administrators must also offer support and freedom to these units, and may find their support, particularly for junior faculty who may be pensive about participation, a key for fostering a new generation of faculty governance leaders.

Note: Special thanks to Dr. Brian Carlisle of the University of California at Los Angeles and Dr. William Patrick Armstrong for their assistance with this chapter.

Chapter 7

Implications for Current Practice

The conversation about faculty involvement in governance rather unfortunately provides no easy answers of right or wrong, but does critically inform best practice and provides a stronger foundation for making big and everyday decisions better. Faculty involvement in governance is at a crossroads for a number of reasons, but perhaps most importantly from two divergent forces: the professionalization of administration and the attitudes of governance board members and state legislatures. The professionalization of administration has gradually eroded the need for a democratic, intellectually driven collegial community. As illustrated in contemporary college athletics and to a lesser extent with university presses, colleges and universities have become very skillful businesses where cost efficiency and profitability outweigh virtually all other institutional culture dimensions. This is also true for externally appointed and elected governing boards who see the college campus as simply another public political game piece much like public utilities and without conscience, manipulate institutional resources for their own gain. And, as attention to public education grows and fosters the idea of K-19, seamless education, it becomes paramount to the history and future of higher education for there to be a forum to defend academic integrity and the mission of higher learning, assuring that in the process of providing education to all that this integrity is not lost.

The lessons generally learned from the NDBFIG project are that faculty governance units, regardless of their nomenclature, tend to hurt themselves more than others who may inhibit their behavior. There are of course exceptions to this, as clearly evidenced in reviewing the Chronicle, and there are very clear questions of power relationships and mutual respect, but broadly, faculty governance units seem to be presenting themselves as amateur administrators with primary regard for the academic life of the institution, but experimenting with virtually every aspect of the college's operation. Whether or not they should be concerned with peripherally-academic issues such as campus green spaces and smoking policies, which certainly do impact the culture of the institution, the messages governance units seem to be sending are confused, mixed agendas. Therefore, if governance units desire more respectability and a different course from what they currently have, they must learn, as an organization that changes from year to year, to become more systematic and purposful in their actions and behaviors. Based on NDBFIG findings, the following recommendations are made to assist governance units and their leaders. A fundamental premise in their offering, however, is that administrative bodies must become partners in the governance process rather than inhibitors, and that in this process, career progression, mission-creep, and public politics take a back seat to institutional welfare. These are certainly substantial assumptions to make, however, they must be addressed in the context of higher learning and the nature of higher education as compared to other mass-marketed commodities.

Practical Implications for Faculty Leaders and Administrators

1. Develop a Future Faculty Senate

Perhaps one of the most consistent challenges for any organization is how to recruit, retain, and motivate a quality group of members. In faculty senates, the challenge is particularly acute in that the body of the membership is typically thrust upon a leader, rather than allowing the leader to hand-pick or select a group to work with. There are, however, a variety of strategies that can be used to develop a stronger group of representative leaders. For those working in a forum setting, these same tactics might be helpful in developing a set of leaders to both serve the future of the unit as well as aiding the current leadership.

- Define the characteristics of the faculty who are most likely to participate and target that audience;
- Design appeals for membership, such as flyers, letters, brochures, public notices, and websites, that appeal to a specific audience;
- Make the benefits of involvement known to the potential senate audience using the most-cost effective methods possible (such as email, if used, and most importantly, personal contact);
- Follow through with offers to senators in a manner that is prompt, accurate, appreciative, and constantly reminds them of the benefits of involvement;
- Regularly provide feedback or evaluation to efforts and individuals recruiting faculty for involvement;
- Change tactics, materials, and structures to meet the changing demands and problems found through evaluation.

Weigand's (1987) six steps refer broadly to any number of organizations that are membership based, but are particularly applicable to faculty groups. First, faculty are primarily rewarded and encouraged to complete other assignments, and involvement in governance is a peripheral identification at best. To lure not just any faculty, but quality faculty leaders, can not be left to chance, yet is rarely the focus of conversation or broad institutional effort.

The difficulty of recruiting faculty senators is often even more difficult due to the election procedures in place at various institutions, and convincing key faculty members not just to participate, but to participate in an election among peers prior to even committing to service on the governance body. At the national level, coalitions of politicians have resulted in parties, and even at the undergraduate level students have found political coalition parties to be helpful in electing slates of student government leaders. With rare exceptions, most likely in situations where those involved with bargaining unit issues are seen informally as an alliance, faculty elections have not taken on the publicity and political rhetoric of similar events.

The key to building a group of action-oriented or change-minded individuals is in taking the time to develop a generic profile of the characteristics of someone who would do well in shared governance (tenured, willing to speak up, assertive, etc.) and then taking the time to meet with the individual and gradually bringing groups of faculty together to talk about what might be and how change can take place. All too often the assumption is made that groups can be assembled in a day or a short period of time, when in reality, particularly in assembling a group that will effect change, the process of identifying and cultivating involvement can take semesters or even years.

2. Foster leadership

Faculty, as highly trained and specialized experts in narrowly defined fields of study can have difficulty arranging operational work into a meaningful agenda that can be advanced. In a sense, those who are collegial, productive, and respected scholars with intellectual depth do not always exhibit the skills and abilities to lead a committee or group of like-minded individuals. There are subsequently few assumptions that faculty senate leaders or administrators can successfully make about work productivity, and by necessity, must learn to become active in preparing committee chairs on a faculty senate to be successful in their work.

Leadership, as a concept, despite it's voluminous reference material and research base, continues to be largely individualistic. Bennis and Nanus (1985) even wrote of leadership, "never have so many labored so long to say so little" (p. 4), and Bass (1990) concluded that the theoretical and conceptual foundations of leadership are heavily fragmented and often disjointed. This means that for faculty and academic senators, there needs to be situationally developed assessments of needed skills and effective training in those skill areas. Assessments might include interviews with committee chairs or key committee members, or perhaps more importantly, by analyzing the work of committees and their leaders to identify underperformance. Resulting areas for skill development might include:

• Meeting and time management
• Group facilitation

- Record keeping (and how to take meeting minutes)
- Group mediation and conflict management
- Creativity development
- How to reward meaningful input
- Problem analysis and diagnosis, and
- Work organization

The most difficult part of fostering leadership among elected faculty representatives is the overriding thought among them that work remain a priority and that basic leadership training is somehow 'beneath' them. This, as might be expected, is an obvious area where administrators must be particularly careful, because if training were to be mandated or even presented in an inappropriate manner, the current adversarial relationship would be made even worse. The responsibility, then, goes to existing faculty leaders who have the authority, belief, respect, and courage to make hard changes for the good of the organization. This task is not simple, and is predicated on fundamentally changing the culture of expectations among governance unit members. The easiest way for this to happen is for elected faculty leaders to begin modeling the behavior expected and placing real, defined, and clear expectations on other elected faculty leaders, such as committee chairs. Some faculty senators may drop out quickly and quietly and some will clearly object, but the courage to change an important organization that represents democratic ideals will not go un-rewarded.

3. Create Systems

Individuals, particularly leading faculty senators and administrators, can have a tremendous impact on the performance of an organization. Indeed, the right leader can transform an organization, but the key to change and continued success is the development of systems, procedures, and institutionalized expectations that will have a long term impact on the role faculty have in decision-making. To do this, faculty leaders must invest time and resources, often their own and with no compensation, in creating an infrastructure to survive long past their involvement. This type of infrastructure might include:

- Creating a complete history of the unit and various committees and minutes
- Creating an accessible tool, such as a website, that allows for
  easily accessible and indexed policies and procedures
- Creating certain rituals, such as orientations, recognition
  awards, transition seminars, and topical lunches that develop
  a cultural appreciation for processes
- Educating (and the routinzation of this education) administrators, deans, chairs, and other faculty about processes and expectations of the faculty governance unit, and
- Adhering to and the discipline to live by the timelines, policies, and culture that the body creates

Change of this nature is substantive and requires strategic, critical thinking about the steps in various tasks and responsibilities.

4. Define an Agenda and Topics

A general strategy that faculty senate leaders have traditionally engaged in for agenda-setting is responsiveness to organizational inertia. Through an informal system of politics and accessi-
bility to the elected leader, an organizational agenda has the ten-
dency to arise naturally. These agenda items often relate to personal concerns rather than constituent concerns, and largely set the
tone for the entire organization's year of work. In some well organized faculty senate settings, committee leaders and elected leadership go on a planning retreat to organize a program of work for
the coming academic year, and some of these will go so far as to
invite campus leaders such as the president, dean, or provost to
attend all or part of the planning session for input on issues to be
addressed and priority setting for work assignments. In some settings, well-organized committees use a final report/goal statement
to provide a record for the new committee chair of issues to be
addressed. Most faculty senates, however, seem to rely on a natural bubbling-up of topics to respond to during the course of the
year.

There is a comprehensive and growing body of literature related to goal and agenda setting, with most focusing on about seven
criteria (Soundview, 1989):

- Plan goals by determining what you want to see happen, and this should be drawn from a number of areas including what is personally valuable;
- Write goals down and share them with many others (including key constituents);
- Make goals specific and obtainable (goals should not be impossible, but they; should be challenging and there should be constant feedback on them);
- Set priorities for the goals and the work necessary to attain them;
- Enjoy reaching goals and reward (even through recognition) to those who help;
- Look at the organization and learn realistically what works and does not work and identify strengths and weaknesses; and
- Keep a positive attitude (often called the most important of personal principles, a positive attitude is composed of faith, optimism, hope, integrity, courage,generosity, tolerance, tact, kindness and good sense).

There is an inter-relationship at work in agenda setting and choosing topics to be dealt with during a year. The relationship involves what the elected leader believes needs to be done, what constituents (aka, faculty, students, staff) think needs to be done, and what institutional leadership wants to have done. Much like an elected congress, the value and importance of the bodies' work is reliant on the selection of important topics and actions that make a difference in the lives of those comprising the academic community. Conversely, manipulation by any one group over an agenda can be negatively seen and can do a great deal to destroy institutional respect (including organizational self-respect). The greatest danger, though, is to do nothing and take on few challenges or few actions, that is unless the senate has conceded to a conceptual stage of serving as a sounding board for faculty voices with no action intended. This level of therapy does have a role in the institution, but certainly is not a method of advancing a topical agenda.

5. Make a Commitment to Representative Training

By using a system of elections, faculty governance units *de facto* commit to a life as a democratic organization. This means that the organization is bound by the ideals of representing the interests of others and not simply the whims or voices of those elected to sit in the senate meeting. The challenge for those elected, then, is how to learn to hear the voices of their constituents, and it is in this regard that faculty governance is generally less sophisticated than student governance. From various institutions around the United States, here is a partial listing of how student governance leaders hear their constituent voices:

- Senators meet with academic unit deans and department chairs;
- Senators have an open meeting once a semester with students in their college/major;
- Senators keep a web-page of issues before the general student government that can impact the college/major;
- Senators visit an academic department every other week during a semester;
- Senators sit at tables in open areas of the college/department, willing to talk to any student who comes by and hear their concerns;
- Senators make announcements at all-college/department faculty meetings;
- Senators visit classes and make a quick announcement about wanting feedback;
- Senators visit student groups affiliated with the college/department and ask for feedback or input about topics or issues to be considered;
- Senators distribute "interest forms" asking for ideas, topics, or issues to be considered, and the interest forms can be submitted anonymously; and
- Student senators meet with faculty senators to discuss issues that might be similarly discussed.

Elected faculty members should at the very least be making announcements to their constituents of issues being considered by the faculty governance unit. With the advent of email and the internet, there is really very little reason why greater communication can not be undertaken. For faculty senate leadership, then, the challenge is to develop a set of habits among faculty senators and a sense of responsibility to share information and gather input about important issues.

6. Find and Invest in Resources

One of the most common topics addressed by faculty governance units is the allocation of resources. Indeed, most public agencies (and even non-profit organizations) struggle with the duality of having to be active and accomplish certain tasks while simultaneously searching for necessary resources. This is particularly true for governance units that are not program-intensive, rather they are reflective, policy oriented bodies that typically have moderate resource requirements (such as Flynn's 2001 listing of office space, secretarial support, etc.). The lack of allocated resources can be a detriment to accomplishing programs of work or unit agendas, and as such, unit leadership must learn to seek additional resources and to use them wisely as investments.

Finding resources in any organization can be challenging, particularly when those resources are highly segmented and often controlled by different personnel. In the college or university this can mean that faculty governance unit members may have no idea or construed right to full resource disclosure (particularly with private, foundation, endowed, or trust accounts, although public budgets do require public disclosure). And even when budgets are disclosed, this does not assure a complete understanding of fund intent and ability for use. Therefore, a good overview and training on the institution's budgeting process and review of various accounting practices is an excellent time investment. Further, by studying the institution, its offices, programs, and structure, governance unit leaders are more apt to be able to identify where funding comes from and what it can be used for. Discretionary funding available for a division of academic affairs, for example, may be rightfully shared with a faculty governance unit to host forums or town hall meetings, and not just to fund projects by a dean of instruction or provost.

In a study of institutional resources, governance unit leaders will also find non-monetary resources that can enable the unit to perform better. One academic senate, for example, developed a strong working relationship with an office of institutional research and effectiveness. The senate could then issue request to that office for reporting information on issues such as workload equity and grade distributions. This data was then considered paramount in future senate debates about creating policy.

An overarching theme for financial resource management at the governance unit level is the responsible use of funding and the professional treatment of resources professionally. Funding also follows performance and good ideas, so governance units may want to consider putting together budgets to be funded from the institution for an entire slate of work to be accomplished rather than asking for sporadic program support. In a sense, the governance unit must convey to the institution that funding is indeed an investment in the institution and not a drain on scarce resources.

7. Establish Networks

A key to accomplishing a program of work is the extent to which governance unit leaders, members, and the organization can handle multiple tasks and assignments. One way to approach the volume of work to be undertaken is through the distribution of assignments among various individuals and offices on campus. The Office of Institutional Research collaboration for data gathering provides a good example of the value of networks on campus. Similarly, a partnership-mentality with Offices of Budget, Computing Services, Development, Student Affairs, and Services, can all prove helpful to a governance unit. In particular, with a primary concern for academic affairs, governance bodies will find networks with student affairs offices to be of great assistance. These are the offices that deal the most directly with students and have vital information on enrollment patterns, retention variables, financial aid and billing cycles, etc.

Networks within the governance unit can also be valuable for a number of reasons, including the acculturation of newer senators or representatives into the organization and to the development of stronger feelings of collaboration for the success of the organization. Additionally, establishing networks among faculty representatives has the potential to break down disciplinary barriers and to maximize the energy and strength of the collective faculty body. Leading this type of organization can be difficult and certainly requires an ego that allows others to succeed and the sharing of recognition. Wheeler (1992) offered three considerations for providing oversight or leadership to an organization that recognizes the collaboration of different members:

- What are the needs and expectations of the senate or governance body? (assess, provide opportunities for input, and do not assume)
- What are the institutional expectations, mission, history, criteria, etc.? (communicate to and among others, do not assume)
- How can the two sets of expectations correlate, interface, and relate? (orchestrate, do not dictate).

These relatively simple questions provide sound advice for leadership among peers: assess with input, communicate openly, do not assume, and do not dictate.

8. Communicate among Leaders

Leadership positions in any organization can be difficult for a variety of reasons. Posing unpopular but responsible actions and behaviors, for example, can lead to harsh feelings and the idea that the actions of the individual are not representative of specific constituents. In senate settings, leadership can often be interpreted as taking an opposing "side," or "siding with administrators." Much like a department chair who must balance actions, behaviors, and language between faculty and administrators, the faculty governance unit leader must balance the interests of the faculty at large, the welfare of the institution, and the interests and activities of administrators. The result is a dramatic need for faculty governance unit leaders to communicate among themselves (such as in executive committees) and among other leaders at the institution.

As Baker (1992) noted, there are indeed normative behavior patterns that demonstrate collaboration, and these simple ideas may prove especially helpful in attempting to work as a team advancing an institution rather than as representatives of special interest groups.

- Pause
- Paraphrase
- Probe for specificity
- Put ideas on the table
- Pay attention to self and others
- Presume positive presuppositions
- Balance advocacy and inquiry

9. Foster Good Senatorship

As a team of individuals with distinct constituents, faculty representatives and unit leaders must find a way to bring out the best in each other. And by encouraging other senators or representatives to speak and act effectively and efficiently, the overall work of the body may be advanced. Hartman (1989) offered a series of questions to define whether an individual is a good group member, and they are relevant to the group member roles of faculty senators:

- Do I ask questions until I have information which will help me to be a more intelligent member of the group?
- Do I try to clarify or interpret the contributions of others until all seem to understand?
- Do I propose new ideas, activities, and procedures?
- Do I make constructive suggestions and evaluations when needed?
- Do I help release the tensions of the group and help create better fellowship between members?
- Do I understand the goals and help the group to keep on track?
- Do I encourage other members to contribute and give them a chance to contribute and ask the group to do so?
- Do I help the group to reach decisions by seeking consensus on a point on which all can agree?
- Do I accept the contributions of others even when I strongly disagree with what they say?
- Do I show concern for the feelings of others and their relation to the group even if this might 'slow down' the work of the group?

10. Commit time to Transitions

As discussed throughout the NDBFIG report, the transition of one set of governance unit leaders to the next is an informal process that probably does not provide for the smoothest of transitions. The transition among faculty leaders is an important process that must include conveying the technical knowledge to be successful along with a cultural understanding of the kinds of issues the body can undertake. Most governance units provide little incentive for transitional programming, and the cost can be quite high: lost time, poor record keeping, the feeling of starting something entirely new, feelings of confusion and disorganization, etc. All of these feelings can similarly be conveyed to the governance body and can immobilize a governance body for weeks or even semesters. Transitional programs need to be more than a turning over of a key or file cabinet, and must include some time committed to mentoring and even on-the-job training. In some instances, administrators are quick to offer friendly advice and these actions can be interpreted to be extensions of manipulative behavior.

Minor (1989) noted that managers have a number of pitfalls to avoid, and many of these mirror those responsibilities and trouble areas for governance unit leaders as they transition between leadership or between academic years. Minor noted that the leader should avoid:

- Thinking you can do everything yourself
- Failing to give senators challenging assignments with enough latitude to handle them
- Careless selection of an authority level when assigning a project
- Holding on to non-management tasks that someone else could do
- Too little or too much follow-up
- Withholding vital information pertinent to a delegated assignment
- Failure to recognize a senator's accomplishments
- Overburdening your best, most trusted people because you have not prepared anyone else
- Failing to hold a critique with a senator after the accomplishment of a major task to see what you both have learned

11. Demand the Respect of Administrators and Governing Board Members

Campbell (2000) provided one of the more cynical representations of what relationships can be like between faculty, administrators, and board members. Indeed, the picture he painted, along with those of Aronowitz, Cesear, and others, demonstrates a very real concern for the respect of faculty members by external bodies. Accrediting bodies similarly seem to be placing increasing demands on the training and performance of faculty members. Campbell's examples of board member intrusion, however, illustrate almost a demonization of faculty by board members. These examples, along with NDBFIG findings, suggest that faculty members must rely only on themselves to assertively demand the respect of administrators and governing board members. Based on the literature cited above, administrators and governing board members seem to have a respect for efficiency and effectiveness, and while both are worthwhile concepts, they are not the measure of success for an academic curriculum and typically those engaged in teaching, research, and service.

Governance units can find elements of respectful behavior by eliminating some of the extraneous conversations that take place in governance bodies, that is, investing time on purely self-serving agendas. Additionally, disorganization of governance unit activities can only add to disrespectful tendencies. So while a governance body need not be as strategic as the business operations of a campus, the procedures of running a governance body need to be fairly clear and well implemented. Similarly, the types and frequency of motions and votes all reflect on governance bodies, so that when a governance body goes two or three years without taking a stance or vote on a substantive issue, it is difficult to claim respect in the eyes of external bodies. The resulting concept to be conveyed, then, is that governance bodies should be responsive to constituent and campus needs, and responsible in their actions.

12. Demand the Respect of Fellow Faculty

Regardless of relationships with external agencies, bodies, and individuals, the core functionality of faculty governance units is the individual faculty member chosen to serve in this body. The individual faculty member has the ability to articulate ideas, concepts, truths, and to take that commitment and turn it into action. The responsibility of the governance unit, then, is to provide a forum for this to take place, an environment where communal ideas, beliefs, and aspirations can be explored and consensus achieved so that action can be pursued, or not pursued, for the welfare of the organization. The need for the governance leader is to create an environment where this exploration and commitment can occur, and a fundamental principle of this environment is a mutual respect for each other among governance unit members. This respect can be furthered through any number of strategies, including the types of committee and work assignments made, the symbolic or ritual recognition of faculty work to the governance unit, the expectations for common treatment of all conveyed by the unit's leadership, and the time outside of formal meetings when governance unit leaders can meet individually with other representatives to develop informal relationships.

Respect among faculty is difficult for a number of reasons, including faculty rank, discipline, academic pedigree, research interests and abilities, and even level of instruction, where those teaching in graduate programs look down upon those who teach in undergraduate programs. These variables all work in contrast to the Dewyian ideal of democracy where there is equality among members of the society. The governance unit is perhaps one of the few places on the college campus where the playing field of representation can be leveled, and this is a reason for extreme optimism in the world of shared governance.

Perhaps the greatest function a faculty governance unit leader can serve is in the creation, maintenance, and furtherance of collegiality. Giamatti (1988) defined collegiality as "the shared sense of a shared set of values, values about open access to information, about open exchange of ideas, about academic freedom, about openness of communication and caring; collegiality is the shared belief, regardless of field or discipline, in a generalized, coherent communal set of attitudes that are collaborative and intellectual. It does not imply unanimity of opinion; it implies commonality of assumption" (p. 39). Collegiality, then, is the culture of the governance unit and the campus at large that creates respect for individuals and empowers faculty to make meaningful decisions and choices for the welfare of all.

Impact on Faculty Involvement in Governance

Colleges and universities have certainly changed, not so much in what they do, but rather in how they fulfill their functions. Giamatti (1988) noted "you will find universities that 10 years ago were run in a collegial fashion now completely structured to look from the outside as if they were manufacturing or banking firmsÖ" (p. 41). Indeed, the very fabric of the college has changed to the extent that faculty roles and responsibilities outside of the classroom are markedly different from two decades ago. There can be any number of instances of finger pointing at various administrators or board members, but the fact remains that institutions will not revert to their ancestral forms of faculty senates (nations) electing proctors. So what does that really mean for the contemporary university? Can faculty governance survive and thrive in this new world of corporate-structured higher education? Current and future faculty members in determining how they choose to be engaged in their professional lives will answer those questions.

As identified throughout the NDBFIG project, faculty members see their governance bodies through many different lenses, and at times, the attention to how the units should be seen supersedes their functioning. The result is a need to invest substantial time from many campus participants in determining communal expectations for shared governance units, and for these units to change with institutions and grow into modern representatives of democracy on campus. Institutions are too large and too complex to rely on a governance body that naively attempts to embrace all of the issues of each academic semester. Instead, faculty senates and councils must be discriminating in deciding what to address, they must be responsive to their constituents, and they must be purposeful in their actions. They must involve many faculty, staff, administrators, and offices to solve problems and defend their rights, while simultaneously serving as a forum for discontent and alternative points of view. As Deming (1986) argued, "put everybody in the company to work to accomplish the transformation. The transformation is everybody's job" (p. 23). The transformation should well be the new higher education institution of the twenty-first century.

Governance unit leaders should also look among themselves for support, encouragement, and in identifying benchmarks or best practice scenarios of how governance bodies can and should work. The internet and the world wide web certainly can play a role in this, and can expose even the most different governance unit leaders to new ideas and different ways of thinking about senate or council behavior. Appendices 1, 2, and 3, all taken from information publicly available on the internet, illustrate the kinds of information available to faculty representatives, administrators, and other governance leaders. Appendix 1 offers the University of Michigan's principles on faculty involvement in institutional and academic governance, and Appendices 2 and 3 are faculty senate by-laws from the University of Alabama and Columbia University, both excellent examples of by-law structures. In Figure 6 are listed additional resources available on the internet for faculty governance unit use. Most of the college and university websites identified here to serve as examples are very comprehensive and are excellent guides for those looking to build resources for governance bodies. The listing is, however, a very small example of those available on the internet.

Faculty involvement in governance does have a foundational purpose and future in higher education, but how this foundation looks and what it is intended to do will continue to change. Twenty years ago, Baldridge (1982) referred to the lost magic kingdom that never was and will not suddenly materialize, so the task before those in faculty governance units is to create a history that will allow future generations of scholars to feel proud of and empowered by. This will require constant refinement, collaboration across disciplines with administrators and trustees, but ultimately will be the defense of academic integrity and the purpose of higher learning.

Figure 6
Internet Sites Providing Exceptional Faculty Governance Information*

Public University Web-Sites

University of Alaska (System) Faculty Alliance
Sygov.swadm.alaska.edu/Faculty/

Robert Holland Faculty Senate at Mississippi State University
Starkville, Mississippi
www.msstate.edu/org/fs/faculty_senate.html

Central Faculty Governance at the University of Michigan
Ann Arbor, Michigan
www.umich.edu/~sacua/index.htm

San Jose State University's Academic Senate
San Jose, California
www.sjsu.edu/senate

Private University Web-Sites

Tulane University's University Senate
New Orleans, Louisiana
www.tulane.edu/%7usenate/

University of Miami's Faculty Senate
Coral Gables, Florida
www.miami.edu/UMH/CDA/UMH_main/1,770,2460-1,00.html

Community College Web-Sites

Cleveland State Community College's Staff Senate (also see
their very good constituent handbook on their website)
Cleveland, Tennessee
www.clevelandstatecc.edu/FacStaff/committees/staff_senate/
index.htm

Figure 6 (*continued*)
Internet Sites Providing Exceptional Faculty Governance
Information*

Shared Governance at DeAnza Community College
Cupertino, California
www.deanza.fhda.edu/faculty/sharedgov/
Associations

American Association of University Professors
www.aaup.org/

National Education Association's Division on Higher Education
www.nea.org/he/

---

*Note: The temporal nature of the internet makes it impossible to
provide definitive web site addresses.

References

Albrecht, D., Carpenter, D. S., & Sivo, S. A. (1994). The effect of college activities and grades on job placement potential. *NASPA Journal, 31*, 290-297.

Altbach, P. G., & Cohen, R. (1989). American student activism: The post-sixties transformation. In P. G. Altbach (Ed.), *Student Political Activism. An International Reference Handbook* (pp. 457-463). New York: Greenwood.

American Association of University Professors. (1966). 1966 statement on government of colleges and universities. Washington, DC: American Association of University Professors.

Armstrong, W. P. (1999). Trends and issues of a community college faculty senate: Jefferson State Community College, 1987-1997. Unpublished doctoral dissertation, University of Alabama, Tuscaloosa.

Arnstein, S. A. (1976). A ladder of citizen participation. In E. Ingram and R. McIntosh (Eds.), *Adaptive Processes in Educational Organizations.* Edmonton: Department of Educational Administration, Faculty of Education, University of Alberta.

Aronowitz, S. (2000). *The knowledge factory, dismantling the corporate university and creating true higher learning.* Boston, MA: Beacon.

Baker, L. (April 30, 2001). Academic senate reflects on productive year. *Daily Nebraskan Online.* Lincoln, NE: University of Nebraska (www.dailynebraskan.com).

Baker, W. (1992). Institute for intelligent behavior. Berkeley, CA.

Baldridge, J. V. (1982). Shared governance: A fable about the lost magic kingdom. *Academic, 68* (1), 12-15.

Bass, B. M. (1990). *Stogdill's handbook of leadership: Theory, research, and managerial applications (3rd. ed.).* New York: Free Press.

Bennis, W., & Nanus, B. (1985). *Leaders.* New York: Harper and Row.

Bergmann, B. (1991). Bloated administration, blighted campuses. *Academe, 77*(6), 12-16.

Birnbaum, R. (1988). *How colleges work.* San Francisco: Jossey-Bass.

Birnbaum, R. (1992). *How academic leadership works: Understanding success and failure in the college presidency.* San Francisco: Jossey-Bass.

Botzek, G. (1972). They got what they asked for. *College Management, 7*(5), 8-10.

Boyer, E. L. (1987). *College: The undergraduate experience in America.* New York: Harper and Row.

Bowen, H. (1980). *The costs of higher education: How much do colleges and universities spend per student and how much should they spend?* San Francisco: Jossey-Bass.

Brown, C., & Miller, M. (1998). Diversity in decision-making: Minority representation in student affairs administration. *College Student Affairs Journal, 18*(1), 25-32.

Cahn, S. M. (1986). *Saints and scamps: Ethics in academia.* Savage, MD: Rowan and Littlefield.

California State Auditor. (2001). *California community colleges: Part-time faculty are compensated less than full-time faculty for teaching activities. Summary of Report No. 2000-107.* Scramento, CA: Author and Bureau of State Audits.

Campbell, J. R. (2000). *Dry rot in the ivory tower.* Lanham, MD: University Press of America.

Cartwright, C. A. (1995). Inquire. Learn. Reflect. The evolution of student activism. *Educational Record, 76*(1), 26-31.

Caesar, T. (2000). Traveling through the boondocks: In and out of academic hierarchy. Albany, NY: State University of New York.

Chronicle of Higher Education. (2001). *Chronicle of Higher Education Almanac 2001-2002.* Washington, DC: Author.

Chronicle of Higher Education. (1995). *Chronicle of Higher Education Almanac 1995-1996.* Washington, DC: Author.

Deming, W. E. (1986). *Out of the crisis.* Cambridge, MA: Massachusetts Institute of Technology, Center for Advanced Engineering.

Dill, D. D., & Helm, K. P. (1988). Faculty participation in strategic policy making. In J. Smart (Ed.), *Higher Education: Handbook of Theory and Research, Vol. 4,* (pp. 319-354). New York: Agathon.

Eliot, C. W. (1908). *University administration.* Boston, MA: Houghton-Mifflin.

Evans, J. P. (1999). Benefits and barriers to shared authority. In M. T. Miller (Ed.), Responsive Academic Decision Making, Involving Faculty in Higher Education Governance, (pp. 29-54). Stillwater, OK: New Forums Press, Inc.

Flynn, J. (2001). Traits of effective faculty senates. Presentation to the National Education Association Critical Issues Seminar on Faculty Involvement in Governance.

French, J. R. P., Jr., & Raven, B. (1959). The bases of social power. In D. Cartwright (Ed.), *Studies in Social Power.* Ann Arbor, MI: Institute for Social Research, University of Michigan.

Fruchter, B. (1954). *Introduction to factor analysis.* Princeton, NJ: Van Nostrand.

Giammatti, A. B. (1988). *A free and ordered space: The real world of the university.* New York: W. W. Norton.

Gilmour, J. (1991). Participative governance bodies in higher education: Report of a national study. In R. Birnbaum (Ed.), *Faculty in Governance: The Role of Senates and Joint Committees in Academic Decision Making. New Directions for Higher Education Report 75* (pp. 27-40). San Francisco: Jossey-Bass.

Gmelch, W., & Burns, J. (1994). Sources of stress for academic department chairpersons. *Journal of Educational Administration, 32,* 79-94.

Goldberg, M. (1980). Student involvement: A resource for administrators. *Educational Record, 61(2),* 15-17.

Gould, J. W. (1968). The academic deanship: A summary and perspective. In A. Dibden (Ed.), *The Academic Deanship in American Colleges and Universities* (pp. 41-56). Carbondale, IL: Southern Illinois University.

Hartman, N. (1989). Group members and group responsibilities. Presentation to Organization and Administration of Higher Education, College of Education, Southern Illinois University at Carbondale.

Hawthorne, E. M. (1991). Anticipating the new generation of community college faculty members. *Journal of College Science Teachers,* 365-368.

Kameras, D. (1996). Teamsters cry foul over UPS team concept. *AFL-CIO News, 41*(4), 5.

Karabell, Z. (1998). *What's college for? The struggle to define American higher education.* NY: Basic.

Katsinas, S., & Kempner, K. (2001). The crisis of leadership development for community colleges: A policy imperative. A White Paper. Denton, TX: Bill J. Priest Center for Community College Education.

Kellogg, A. P. (May 18, 2001). Faculty senate at Notre Dame, angry over lackof clout, votes to dissolve. *Chronicle of Higher Education,* 47(36), A14.

Kerr, C. (1991). *The great transformation in higher education.* Albany, NY: State University of New York.

Laabs, T. R. (1987). Community college tenure: Teach or research? *Community/ Junior College Quarterly, 11,* 267-273.

Lucas, C.J. (2000). *American higher education a history.* New York: St. Martin's Green.

Maehr, M. L., & Braskamp, L. A. (1986). *The motivation factor.* Lexington, MA: Lexington.

Martin, J., Samels, J. E., & Associates. (1997). *First among equals: The role of the chief academic officer.* Baltimore, MD: Johns Hopkins University.

McConnell, T. R., & Mortimer, K. P. (1971). The faculty in university governance. Berkeley, CA: Center for Research and Development in Higher Education, University of California.

McCormack, T. F. (1995). A study of governance in higher education in the State of Alabama. Unpublished doctoral dissertation, University of Alabama, Tuscaloosa, AL.

McCroskey, J. C. (1977). Oral communication apprehension: A summary of recent theory and research. *Human Communication Research, 4*(1), 78-93.

McCroskey, J. C., & Sheahan, M. E. (1978). Communication, social preference, and social behavior in a college environment. *Communication Quarterly, 26*(20), 41-45.

Michener, J. A. (1971). *Kent State: What happened and why.* New York: Random House.

Michener, J. A. (1985). *Texas.* NY: Fawcett Crest.

Miles, A. S. (1997A). *College law (2ⁿᵈ ed.).* Tuscaloosa, AL: Sevgo.

Miles, J. M. (1997B). Student leader perceptions of increasing participation in self-governance. Unpublished doctoral dissertation, University of Alabama, Tuscaloosa, AL.

Miles, R.E. (1965). Human relations or human resources? *Harvard Business Review, 43*(4), 148-155.

Miller, M. T. (1998). Student affairs task force on the effectiveness of the reconstituted student government association. Unpublished Task Force Report, Division of Student Affairs, University of Alabama, Tuscaloosa, AL.

Miller, M. T., & Nelson, G. M. (1996). Student cultures on campus: Priorities for a decade of research. Paper presented at the International Conference in Popular Culture, Honolulu, HI.

Miller, M. T., & Seagren, A. T. (1993). Faculty leader perceptions of improving participation in higher education governance. *College Student Journal, 27,* 112-188.

Miller, M., T., Williams, C., & Garavalia, B. J. (forthcoming). Path analysis and power rating in communication channels in a faculty senate setting. In M. Miller and J. Caplow (Eds) *Policy and Faculty Governance.* Norwood, NJ: Ablex.

Minor, M. (1989). *Coaching and counseling: A practical guide for managers.* Crisp Publications.

Mortimer, K. (1974). Research data on tenure and governance under collective bargaining. Speech delivered at the Annual Meeting of the American Federation of Teachers, New York, NY.

Mortimer, K. P., & McConnell, T. R. (1978). *Sharing authority effectively: Participation, interaction, and discretion.* San Francisco: Jossey-Bass.

Murphy, P. J. (1991). A collaborative approach to professional development. *Education Research and Perspectives, 18*(1), 59-65.

Nelson, C. A. P., & McCroskey, J. C. (1989). *Communication apprehension, avoidance, and effectiveness (2ⁿᵈ ed.).* Scottsdale, AZ: Corsuch Scarisbrick.

Rojstaczer, S. (1999). *Gone for good, tales of university life after the golden age.* New York: Oxford University.

Rosovsky, H. (1990). *The university an owner's manual.* New York: W. W. Norton.

Schlesinger, S., & Baldridge, J. V. (1982). Is student power dead in higher education? *College Student Journal, 16,* 9-17.

Scroggs, S. (1949). Administration and organization. In P. F. Valentine (Ed.), *The American College* (pp. 433-471). NY: Philosophical Library.

Seagren, A., Wheeler, D., Creswell, J., Miller, M., & VanHorn-Grassmeyer, K. (1994). *Academic leadership in community colleges.* Lincoln, NE: University of Nebraska.

Selingo, J. (May 19, 2000). In Pennsylvania, a powerful crusader pushes universities to change their ways. *Chronicle of Higher Education, 47,* A35.

Shapiro, J. (November 16, 2001). Winning tenure, losing the thrill. *Chronicle of Higher Education, 48,* B7.

Shults, C. (2001). *The critical impact of impending retirements on community college leadership. AACC Leadership Series No. 1.* Washington, DC: American Association for Community Colleges.

Sims, R. A. (1998). Shared governance – a wasteful exercise? *Administrator, 17*(3), 3.

Soundview. (1989). *Skills for success, the experts show the way.* Middlebury, VT: Soundview Publishers.

Taylor, F. W. (1967). The principles of scientific management. New York: W. W. Norton & Company.

Trow, M. L. (1990). The academic senate. *Liberal Education, 76*(1), 23-27.

Twombly, S. B. (1988). Administrative labor markets. *Journal of Higher Education, 59*(6), 668-689.

University of Michigan. (1977) Principles of faculty involvement in institutional and academic unit governance at the University of Michigan. Retrieved online at www.umich.edu/~sacua/AcadAff/aaacdoc.html on July 3, 2001.

Weber, M. (1947). *The theory of social and economic organizations.* New York: Free Press.

Weigand, C. (1987). *Membership development handbook.* Washington, DC: The Taft Group.

Westerfield, R. C. (1997). Personal communication. Tuscaloosa, AL: University of Alabama.

Wheeler, D. (1992). Balancing career and personal life. Presentation to the Institute for Agricultural and Natural Resources, University of Nebraska-Lincoln.

Wildavsky, A. (1988). *The new politics of the budgetary process.* Glenview, IL: Scott, Foresman, and Company.

Williams, D., Gore, W., Broches, C., & Lostoski, C. (1987). One faculty's perceptions of its governance role. *Journal of Higher Education, 58,* 629-655.

Williams, M., & Winston, R. B. (1985). Participation in organized student activities and work: Differences in developmental task achievement of traditional aged college students. *NASPA Journal, 22*(3), 52-59.

Williamson, B. (1984). Students, higher education, and social change. *European Journal of Education, 19,* 253-267.

APPENDIX 1

Unanimously endorsed by the Provost and the Senate Assembly on April 21, 1997

The University of Michigan Aacademic Affairs Advisory Committee

A Report to the Senate Assembly from the members of the Academic Affairs Advisory Committee

INTRODUCTION TO GENERAL PRINCIPLES OF FACULTY PARTICIPATION IN GOVERNANCE

At the request of the Provost, the Academic Affairs Advisory Committee proposes the following statement of general principles for faculty participation in institutional and academic unit governance. These principles are based, in part, on Sec. 5.02, Sec. 5.03, and Sec. 5.04 of the University of Michigan Bylaws of the Board of Regents, and upon recommendations for the government of colleges and universities as set forth by the American Council on Education, the Association of Governing Boards of Universities and Colleges, and the American Association of University Professors.

Faculty participation in governance promotes and encourages diversity of ideas, a sense of shared responsibility, collaboration, collegiality, and institutional excellence. The faculty of the University of Michigan is encouraged to use these principles as a basis for the development of means for participation in governance in all units.

I. General Principles for Faculty Participation in Institutional Governance

1. The faculty has primary responsibility for such fundamental areas as curriculum, subject matter and methods of instruction, research, faculty status, standards and procedures for admission of students, and those aspects of student life which relate to the educational process.

2. The faculty sets the degree requirements, determines when the requirements have been met, and otherwise qualifies students and recommends them to the president and Board of Regents to grant the degrees thus achieved.

3. Considerations of faculty status and related matters are primarily a faculty responsibility; this area includes matters relating to academic titles, appointments, reappointments, decisions not to reappoint, promotions, the recommending of tenure and dismissal. Policies and procedures shall be developed for the implementation for these faculty responsibilities.

4. The faculty shall participate in the determination of policies and procedures governing compensation of faculty.

5. Agencies for faculty participation in the government of the college/school or university shall be established at each level where faculty responsibility is to be met. A faculty-elected campus-wide body shall exist for the presentation of the views of the whole faculty.

    The agencies may consist of meetings of all faculty members of a department, school, college, division, or university system, or they may take the form of faculty-elected executive committees in departments and colleges/schools, and a faculty-elected body for larger divisions or for the institution as a whole.

6. Budgetary policies and decisions directly affecting those areas for which the faculty has primary responsibility — such as, but not limited to, curriculum, subject matter and methods of instruction, research, faculty status, admission of students and those aspects of student life which relate to the educational process shall be made in concert with the faculty.

7. The preceding faculty responsibilities remain in effect when there is a delegation of faculty governance to agencies or administrative officers. Faculty must exercise diligence and provide oversight to ensure that its agencies act in keeping with its policies and recommendations, and that they are implemented in an appropriate manner.

II. Academic Unit Level Governance: Principles

1. Although the principles of governance apply to all academic units the forms of faculty governance may vary among units.
2. Every academic unit at the University of Michigan shall have a set of written rules and procedures for its governance, copies of which are to be available to each faculty member.
3. The governing faculty of each academic unit shall establish the responsibilities and authority of each academic unit governance entity and each administrative entity within that unit. This applies to the lines of decision-making authority of these entities in relation to: curriculum; admission requirements; graduation requirements; major operating procedures such as departmental organization, committee organization, committee appointments; budget; faculty appointments, reappointments, decisions not to reappoint; faculty promotion and tenure; and policies concerning reviews of faculty for merit salary increases.
4. The governing faculty of each academic unit shall establish the operating procedures of its academic unit governance entities including, but not limited to: procedures for agenda setting, establishment of a quorum, determination of membership and voting rights, qualification of attendance by persons other than members, appointment of a faculty secretary, distribution of minutes, and the retention/filing of minutes.
5. For those academic units where the faculty delegates authority to an executive committee the following principles apply:
   a. Procedures for nomination and election of executive committee members shall be determined by the governing faculty of the unit.

b. All recommendations to the Regents concerning a unit executive committee or other unit governance entity shall be based on a vote of the governing faculty of the unit.
c. The governing faculty shall establish the membership criteria for the executive committee with consideration for balance among various components of the unit, such as unit programs and departments, to make the executive committee representative of the governing faculty of the unit.
d. The governing faculty shall establish criteria for those eligible to serve on the executive committee, e.g. membership in the governing faculty or in the professional faculty, fraction of appointment, and holding of administrative positions.
e. The governing faculty shall establish policies and procedures by which a vote by secret ballot among nominees for membership on the executive committee will be conducted, and for the transmission of the names of those elected to the Regents.
f. The governing faculty shall establish policies and procedures to be used to fill a vacancy if a member of the executive committee must take a leave of absence or is otherwise unable to complete the original term of office.
g. The governing faculty shall establish policies and procedures regarding the term of office of elected member and any other restrictions on terms of office.

APPENDIX 2

Sample Faculty Senate By-Laws from
The University of Alabama

Article I. Senate Officers

In all elections of Senate Officers-President, Vice President, and
Secretary-elections will be by the vote of the majority of the
senators voting, in a meeting at which a quorum of the Senate is
present. Nominations and election of the Senate President will be
completed before the floor is opened for nominations for Vice
President, and the election of the Vice President will be made
before nominations are received for the Office of Secretary. Any
senator interested in serving in one or more of these offices may
submit a written statement of intention, with any supporting
argument, not to exceed one page in length, to the Secretary of
the Senate by March 14 of the year in which he or she hopes to
commence office. The Secretary will distribute each such
statement and supporting argument with the agenda for the
March meeting of the Senate. Persons may also be nominated for
these offices from the floor at the March meeting. A motion to
close nominations, or the equivalent, is out of order. Each
candidate will have an opportunity to speak to the Senate about
his or her candidacy, and the Senate will have an opportunity to
ask questions of each candidate.

Article II. Organization

Section 1. Senate Orientation.

There will be an orientation session for all new Senators and Alternates on the first Tuesday in April that the University is in session. This will be an occasion for discussion of the history and the place of the Senate in the governance of the University, of the role and function of the Senate's officers, of the charge and function of the Senate's standing committees, and of other aspects of the Senate Constitution and Bylaws. Before the first regular meeting of the new Senate, there will also be a social function at which Senators and Alternates may become more fully acquainted with each other.

Section 2. Steering Committee.

The Steering Committee is authorized to make representations in its own name in regard to any matter within the scope of the Senate's responsibilities and functions (as defined in Article II of the Constitution) when, in the Committee's judgment, circumstances require action before it is possible to convene a meeting of the Senate. In such instances, the Committee will be guided by its best judgment regarding the intention of the Senate if such intention is known.

Section 3. Standing Committees.

1. There shall be standing committees on:
    • Academic Affairs (11)
    • Financial Affairs (9)
    • Planning and Operations (5)
    • Research and Service (5)
    • Student Affairs (5)
    • Senate Operations (3)

2. Subject to reasonable exceptions to accommodate the needs of the Senate and the interests of senators, each senator ordinarily will have one standing committee assignment. The number of members shall be approximately that indicated in parentheses for the respective committees.

3. After the orientation session and social occasion described in Section 1, the Secretary will ask each Senator to list preferences for assignment to the Senate's standing committees. After consultation with those who served as chairs of standing committees the previous year, the Secretary will assign each Senator to his or her first choice, if possible, and using second or third preferences where first preferences are unavailable. Senators who have indicated no preference by the second Tuesday in April shall be assigned to committees by the Secretary. All such assignments are subject to the approval of the Senate. The Secretary will distribute the tentative assignment of Senators to committees with the agenda for the regular April meeting. The first order of business for the regular April meeting will be to debate the assignment of Senators to committees, to reassign if necessary, and to confirm the final assignment by vote of the Senate. The President of the Senate will thereupon name convenors for each of the standing committees, and following the close of the regular April meeting each convenor will hold a brief meeting of each standing committee for purposes of establishing a place for meeting, if necessary, before the next scheduled meeting of the Senate steering committee. By the end of April, each standing committee will elect a chair or co-chairs from among its membership; if a chair is selected it may elect a vice-chair. Each chair or co-chair of a standing committee serves as a full member of the steering committee. Each standing committee will normally meet on the first Tuesday of each month from September through November and January through March, and at other times as desirable.

4. Standing committees will inform themselves, on their own initiative or pursuant to specific instructions from the Senate, concerning matters of current concern within their respective jurisdictions. Standing committees, directly or through their chairs are expected to seek and maintain continual dialogues with the vice presidents in charge of the areas of University affairs in which the respective committees have jurisdiction. Monthly meetings are an example of a mechanism for such dialogues. The committees shall make such reports and rec-

ommendations to the Senate as they deem appropriate or as
the Senate requires.

5. Senators are expected to attend meetings of their standing committees. The absence of a Senator from a regularly scheduled
committee meeting may be referred by the chair or co-chair
of the committee to the Senate Operations Committee. Senators who regularly fail to attend committee meetings and do
not provide for the attendance of alternates may be replaced
on the committee.

6. Committee on Academic Affairs. The Academic Affairs Committee is responsible for considering issues which relate to
instruction, curriculum, academic standards, academic freedom, collegiality, tenure and promotion, and other issues which
directly affect the learning environment of the University and
the quality of its intellectual life. Questions relating directly
to research and service, financial issues, and student issues
will, however, normally be referred to the appropriate committee of the Faculty Senate.

7. Committee on Financial Affairs. The Financial Affairs Committee reviews financial issues that are pertinent to the University community and makes recommendations to the Faculty Senate concerning these issues.

8. Committee on Student Affairs. The Student Affairs Committee advises the Faculty Senate on issues related to the social
and academic development of students.

9. Committee on Research and Service. The Research and Service Committee is charged with studying and making recommendations on matters that affect the research and service component of faculty life.

10. Committee on Planning and Operations. The Planning and Operations Committee studies the allocation of resources within
the University and works to ensure communication between
faculty and administration in relation to resource policies and
allocations, advances proposals consistent with Faculty Senate initiatives and priorities, and makes recommendations to
the Faculty Senate pertaining to resource policies and allocations.

11. Committee on Senate Operations.

   a. The Committee on Senate Operations is responsible for continuous review of the Senate's organization and procedures and for recommending changes it deems desirable in either the Constitution or the Bylaws.

   b. The Senate Operations Committee will consider the reasonableness of all absences in excess of two by a senator from Senate meetings in which the senator is not represented by a duly elected alternate and will make a recommendation to the Senate whether the position should be declared vacant. The Operations Committee also will be responsible for determining if a Senate seat is vacant for reasons other than absence and will make appropriate recommendations to the Senate.

   c. The Senate Operations Committee is responsible for interpreting the Constitution and Bylaws and may receive requests for interpretation from the Senate or the Senate President or may initiate action by itself. All such interpretations must be reported to the Senate and are subject to Senate concurrence.

   d. The Senate Operations Committee is charged with responsibility for determining the constitutionality of the Senate Bylaws. Such determinations must be reported to the Senate and are subject to Senate concurrence.

Section 4. Special Committees.

Special committees may be created by the Senate as needed. Unless the Senate directs otherwise, special committee members and chairpersons shall be designated by the same methods as for standing committees. Persons eligible to vote in Senate elections who are not members of the Senate may be appointed by special committees as their consultants.

Section 5. Subcommittees.

Standing and special committees may establish such standing or special subcommittees as they deem useful. Persons eligible to vote in Senate elections who are not members of the Senate may be appointed by subcommittees as their consultants.

Section 6. Parliamentarian.

The Senate President will nominate a parliamentarian, subject to Senate confirmation, to serve as recommended in the most recent revision of Robert's Rules of Order except where these Rules are contravened by a rule adopted by the Senate. This person will be a member of the Faculty, as defined in the Constitution, who is not a senator; or a member of the retired faculty. It shall be the duty of the Parliamentarian to attend all meetings of the Senate and of the Steering Committee.

Section 7. Webmaster.

The Senate President will nominate a webmaster, subject to Senate confirmation, to serve as the producer and coordinator of the Senate's web site. This person will be a member of the faculty, who may be but need not be a senator.

Section 8. Offices.

The Senate shall maintain offices, in a room or rooms in the University assigned by the President of the University. The Senate offices shall be the location of the files of the Senate.

Article III. Procedures

Section 1. Meeting (Senate and Steering Committee).

1.   The Senate will meet on the third Tuesday, August through November and January through April, and the second Tuesday of December, at 3:30 p.m. in locations to be determined by the Steering Committee. If the third Tuesday falls during a time when the University is not in session, the Senate will meet on the second or fourth Tuesday, as the Steering Committee determines, and the meetings of Senate committees may have to be adjusted appropriately. The Senate may meet also on the fourth Tuesday, August through November and January through April, and the third Tuesday in December, in order to finish the business of the month, and Senators should keep this date free on their calendars. The Senate will also meet at other times, including the summer months, and at locations, as decided by the Senate or the Steering Committee.

The regular meeting times and locations shall be decided for the upcoming year by the Steering Committee at its August meeting, Senators will be appropriately notified, and the information will be published in Dialog and/or other publications deemed useful.

2. Regular Senate meetings normally last until 5:00 and may last longer. Senators should clear their calendars until 5:15 on regular Senate meeting days upon such an expectation. Senators are expected to maintain their attendance until 5:00, or until the meeting is adjourned prior thereto.

3. The Steering Committee will hold a regular meeting one week before each regularly scheduled meeting of the Senate. Special meetings of the Steering Committee may be called by the President of the Senate, by the written request of three members of the Steering Committee or of five members of the Senate, by vote of the Steering committee, or by vote of the Senate.

4. All resolutions and original motions to be presented to the Senate must be in writing and should be mailed by the Senate Secretary with the agenda for the meeting.

5. A majority of members shall constitute a quorum. A quorum must be present before any vote can be taken.

Section 2. Agenda.

1. Except when the Steering Committee or the Senate orders otherwise, the customary order of business as described in Robert's Rules of Order will be followed.

2. The agenda will be distributed to members during the week in advance of the meetings by the Senate Secretary except when exigent circumstances make it necessary, in the judgment of the Steering Committee, to prepare or change an agenda so soon before the meeting that advance circulation is impractical.

3. The Steering Committee will employ whatever means are feasible and appropriate to give notice of pending agenda items to all members of the Senate.

4. The agenda will be placed on the Senate's web page and will

contain sufficient information, both in summary or "bullet" form and in detail, so that the issues to be debated in the Senate are clear. Each person or committee that propounds a motion or submits a report to be included in or with the agenda is responsible for providing a succinct summary of the issue(s) involved. The President's Report, reports from the standing committees, and reports from Senators about the activity of University committees should be included with the agenda if at all possible, so as to reduce the time used in Senate meetings for explanation and summary. The minutes of each meeting also will be placed on-line in "bullet" form, and in detail on the Senate's web page. Other documents of interest to faculty and/or pertinent to issues being debated in the Senate may also be placed on the Senate's web page.

Section 3. Access to Senate Meetings.

1.   Any person may attend Senate meetings during other-than-executive sessions for the purpose of observing its proceedings.

2.   Anyone other than a senator may address the Senate only on invitation by vote of the Senate or on invitation by the President of the Senate after an opportunity for the Senate to object and, in case there is objection, alter approval of the invitation by the Senate.

3.   An executive session, from which all persons except senators are excluded, may be held by vote of the Senate. Motions to hold executive sessions will take precedence over other regular business.

4.   The privilege of the floor, including the right to address the Senate on any pending question subject to applicable rules or parliamentary procedure, and non-voting membership on the Steering Committee, are extended to one delegate representing the Retired Faculty Association of The University of Alabama, one delegate representing the Professional Staff Committee, one delegate representing the Office/Clerical/Technical Staff Committee, one delegate representing the Maintenance personnel Committee, one delegate representing the

Student Government Association, and one delegate representing the Office of Alumni Affairs.

Section 4. Minutes of Senate Meetings.

1. Minutes of all Senate meetings shall be furnished to all senators as early as possible.
2. Copies of minutes of open Senate meetings are to be freely available to anyone within or without the University of Alabama: first, within the University; second, outside the University on request and if available.
3. Divisional delegations are expected to adopt measures for effective and expeditious reporting of Senate actions to their constituencies.
4. The official minutes of all open Senate meetings shall be available for inspection by all persons eligible to vote in the election of senators. The official minutes of executive sessions of the Senate shall be made available for this purpose only to the extent as the Senate may approve.
5. Minutes of executive sessions of the Senate are confidential and are not to be released.
6. Minutes of the Steering Committee may be made available outside the University of Alabama only by a majority vote of the Steering Committee that is asked for such material.
7. Reports submitted to the Senate become part of the open-meeting minutes or executive-session minutes and are to be treated as those minutes.

Section 5. Committee Records.

1. All Senate committees shall keep records of their meetings and proceedings, describing in summary form all noteworthy matters considered and noting all committees and actions.

Section 6. Additional Responsibilities of the Senate Secretary.

1. The Secretary has responsibility for conducting all University-wide referenda regarding proposed amendments to the Constitution.

2. The Secretary is charged with keeping the official, up-to-date copies of the Constitution and Bylaws, and with assuring that a signed and dated notification of official approval by the Secretary is affixed to all copies of the Constitution and Bylaws.
3. The Secretary will call the roll of senators at each meeting of the Senate. Any absences in excess of two by a senator will be reported by the Secretary to the Senate Operations Committee.
4. It shall be a duty of the Senate Secretary to notify the deans of the divisions of the University of the need for regular and special elections of senators. In so doing, the Secretary will note the name of the Senator who previously held the position or of the need to elect additional senators.
5. It shall be the duty of the Senate Secretary to publish a calendar of Senate meetings for the academic year at the beginning of each fall semester. It shall contain the times and locations of Senate meetings and the listing of the dates upon which the Senate must take actions such as the naming of members of official bodies of the University or the appointment of committees to nominate award recipients.

Section 7. Senate Appointments to University Committees.

The following procedures apply to the appointments made under authority given to the Faculty Senate by the University's Faculty Handbook, or by the President of the University, or by other University authority:

1. Senators shall be asked in the spring by the Secretary for their preferences of service on University standing committees. The President, assisted by the Vice President and the Secretary, shall tentatively assign Senators to University standing committees, giving as much weight as possible to the preferences they have communicated. Such tentative assignments shall be discussed, and modified if necessary, by the Steering Committee, and shall be submitted to the whole Senate for discussion, modification if necessary, and approval, before the list is timely transmitted to the President of the University.

2. All other University committee or task force appointments in the gift of the Faculty Senate, including appointments to search committees or review committees, shall be made by the President of the Senate in consultation, if possible, with the Steering Committee, and shall be communicated to the Senate at its next meeting. If time does not allow for such consultation at a regular meeting of the Steering Committee, the President may call a meeting of that Committee or, in an emergency, poll the Committee by telephone, by e-mail, in person, or in other available ways; at least two-thirds of the Committee must be polled. In the latter instance, the whole Steering Committee may, at its next meeting, refuse to confirm the appointee, in which situation another appointment must be made, subject to consultation with the Steering Committee.

Article IV. Amendments of Bylaws

The Bylaws may be amended by a majority vote of the members of the Senate at a meeting subsequent to the meeting at which the amendment
was proposed.

I certify that this is a correct and accurate copy of the Bylaws of the Faculty Senate of the University of Alabama.

April 18, 2000

APPENDIX 3

BY LAWS OF THE FACULTY SENATE AT
COLUMBIA UNIVERSITY

Sec. 1: ORGANIZATION AND PROCEDURE

a. Rules. Subject to the provision of these By-Laws, the Senate shall establish its own rules of procedure.

b. Presiding Officer. The President of the University shall be the presiding officer of the Senate. In his absence, or at his request, the Chairman of the Executive Committee shall preside as Speaker pro tempore.

c. Meetings. The Senate shall hold regular meetings at least once a month during the academic year, and may meet more frequently by decision of a majority of its members present and voting, at the call of the President of the University at the call of the Executive Committee, or at the call of one-third of all its members. Meetings of the University Senate shall be open to members of the University community, campus press, radio and other campus news media, unless such meetings have been designated closed by the Executive Committee of the Senate and such designation has not been overruled by a majority of the members of the Senate present and voting thereon.

d. Quorum. One-half of the membership of the Senate shall constitute a quorum for the conduct of the Senate's business.

e. Agenda. The Senate shall prepare its own agenda, and the Executive Committee of the Senate shall serve as the agenda committee. The Senate's agenda shall include all matters referred to the Senate by its various standing and special committees, and all matters within its jurisdiction that may be referred to it by the President, the Trustees, or the Executive Committee itself. A majority of the members of the Senate may place an item on the agenda at any time.

f. Introduction of Proposals. Any senator may introduce proposals, including measures and resolutions, from the floor of the Senate. Such proposals shall be referred to the appropriate committee to be dealt with in accordance with Senate rules.

g. Floor Privileges. The Dean or Director of any Faculty, School, or Administrative Board, whether or not he is a senator, shall have the right to speak and participate in debate whenever any matter that is of special concern to his particular Faculty or School is before the Senate.

The student body in each of the following affiliated institutions may elect one or two student observers, with Teachers College eligible to elect two, and Union Theological Seminary eligible to elect one. If any of the affiliated institutions elect such student observers, they shall be entitled to sit with the University Senate but shall not vote or otherwise participate in its deliberations, unless particular questions relevant to student interests in affiliated institutions are the subject of Senate action, in which case, with the approval of the Chairman, they shall have a voice but not a vote.

When the Senate considers the report of any standing committee of the Senate, or of any committee, commission, or other group appointed by the Senate or by the Senate Executive Committee, members of that standing committee, and members of such committees, commissions, or groups, who are not members of the Senate may sit with the Senate and have a voice but not a vote in the deliberations of the Senate on that report.

h. Committee Reports: Discharge of Committees. The majority of the members of any committee of the Senate may report on any matter before the committee. A majority of the members of the Senate present and voting may require a committee to report at the next regular meeting of the Senate, and one-third of the members of the Senate present and voting may require the committee to report no later than the second regular meeting of the Senate next following.

i.   Petitions for Senate Action. Any matter may be placed on the agenda of any appropriate committee of the Senate as determined by the Executive Committee by petition signed by 150 members of the University community who are entitled to vote for members of the Senate. Any Committee on Instruction may place a matter on the agenda of an appropriate committee shall be disposed of by the committee at the earliest time with due regard to other prior agenda items, and the disposition shall be reported to the full University Senate.

j.   Minutes. The Minutes of the Senate shall be widely disseminated, and shall be made available to the campus and other news media. Copies of the Minutes shall be posted in at least two prominent places on the Morningside Campus and at least one prominent place in each of the divisions of the University not on the Morningside Campus.

Sec. 2: FINALITY OF SENATE ACTION; CONCURRENCE BY TRUSTEES; AMENDMENT OF BY-LAWS.

a.   Action of the Senate shall become final on first passage unless Trustee concurrence is necessary pursuant to Section 25 of the Statutes of the University.

b.   Notwithstanding the provisions of sub-section (a), the President of the University may convene a special meeting of the Senate within 15 class days of any Senate action, and may request it to reconsider such action.

c.   The provisions of these By-Laws shall not be subject to amendment except by a three-fifths vote of all incumbent members of the Senate.

Sec. 3: COMMITTEES

    a.   Establishment. There shall be the following standing committees:

Executive Committee
Committee on Education
Committee on Rules of University Conduct
Committee on Budget Review
Committee on Alumni Relations
Committee on Honors and Prizes
Committee on Libraries and Academic Computing Facilities
Committee on Physical Development of the University
Committee on Student Affairs
Committee on Faculty Affairs, Academic Freedom and Tenure
Committee on Senate Structure and Operations
Committee on External Relations and Research Policy

    b.   Additional Committees. Such additional standing and special committees may be established from time to time as deemed necessary.

    c.   Periodic Reorganization of the Senate. The regular organization of the Executive Committee and other standing committees of the Senate and elections of committee chairmen shall take place biennially, in odd calendar years, following the spring election.

    Each outgoing Senate committee which considers that it has continuing business to be conducted in the summer interim may so advise the incoming Executive Committee and request it, under the Senate's delegation of summer powers, to appoint interim committees as necessary to conduct this business until the new committees are constituted, and include in their membership such members of the outgoing committee as are available for service.

    d.   Responsibility. Every committee of the Senate shall operate within the area of its jurisdiction as an arm of the Senate and, except where expressly indicated otherwise in these By-Laws, committees shall be responsible to the Senate and shall report recommendations for consideration and action by the Senate as a whole.

e. Committee Membership. Except as otherwise expressly provided in this section, persons who are not members of the Senate may serve as members of Senate committees. At least a majority of every committee shall, however, be senators. The membership of several committees, other than the Executive Committee, shall be elected as follows: each member of the Senate shall submit to the Executive Committee the first three choices for committee service in the order of his preference; the Executive Committee shall then nominate the membership of each committee so that, to the fullest extent possible, no member of the Senate is nominated to a committee that is not among his first three choices; after the Executive Committee has made its nomination, nominations from the floor shall be in order, and the Senate as a whole shall elect the members of each committee by majority vote.

f. Committee Chairmen. Each committee, other than the Executive Committee, shall elect its chairman from among its members.

g. Absences. If a member has more than two consecutive unexcused absences from committee meetings scheduled at least one week in advance, the seat shall be deemed vacant. Each committee shall determine the grounds for absence from its meetings. When a member shall have accumulated two consecutive unexcused absences, the chairman of the committee shall notify the member and the Executive Committee. The Executive Committee may recommend to the Senate that the member be continued on the committee, or it may nominate a new member. The Senate as a whole shall reappoint the member or elect a new member by a majority vote.

h. The composition and jurisdiction of the several standing committees shall be as follows:

1. Executive Committee

The Executive Committee shall consist of 13 members apportioned as follows: 6 tenured faculty, 2 non-tenured faculty, 2 administrators, and 3 students. All shall be members of the Senate. The two administration representatives shall be the President and another officer of administration of his choice. Elected members of the Executive Committee shall be chosen as follows: each category in the Senate entitled to members on the Executive Committee as here provided shall nominate the requisite number and the membership of the Senate as a whole shall vote on each of the nominees; a nominee who receives a majority of the total number of affirmative votes cast shall become a member of the Executive Committee; if a nominee fails to achieve a majority, the category that nominated him shall nominate another person in his stead. Following the election of the Executive Committee, the Chairman of the Committee shall be nominated and elected from among the tenured faculty members by the Senate as a whole.

The Executive Committee shall be the Senate's agenda committee and its committee on committees. It may authorize standing committees without regular and recurring duties, if they request to be put on a stand-by basis, to meet once a semester and otherwise be on the call of the Senate or the Executive Committee or of a majority of the Committee concerned as the need for the activity of such committees may arise. The Executive Committee shall have the power to call the Senate into extraordinary session, and shall have such powers, functions and duties as the Senate may delegate to it during periods when the Senate is not in session. The Executive Committee shall serve as a continuing liaison between the University Senate and the central administration. The Executive Committee may create subcommittees and may delegate any of its powers, functions, and duties. The Executive Committee shall participate pursuant to the Statutes of the University and the By-Laws of the Trustees, in the selection of University Professors, the President of the University, the Provost or Provosts, and six Trustees. In performing these functions, the Executive Committee or the appropriate subcommittee thereof shall act in executive session and in a confidential manner and shall not be required to report its deliberations or actions to the Senate as a whole.

To the extent possible, officers of instruction may be allowed a reduction in their teaching loads and students may be granted appropriate credit for serving as members of the Executive Committee.

2. Committee on Education

The Committee on Education shall consist of 19 members apportioned as follows: 8 tenured faculty, 3 non-tenured faculty, 4 students, 2 administrators, 1 alumnus and 1 library staff. The Committee on Education shall review, and may from time to time recommend, plans and policies relating to the educational system of the University. The Committee shall receive ideas, recommendations, and plans for educational innovations from members of the faculty and others. The Committee shall inform itself of conditions in the several schools, faculties and departments, and propose measures needed to make the most effective use of the resources of the University for educational purposes.

3. Committee on Budget Review

The Committee on Budget Review shall consist of 11 members, all of whom shall be members of the Senate. The membership of the Committee shall consist of 5 tenured faculty representatives, 2 non-tenured faculty, 2 student representatives, 1 alumnus and the Chairman of the Executive Committee or his designee serving ex officio. The Budget Review Committee shall review the annual budget of the University after its adoption to assure its general conformity with short-range and long-range priorities of the University and expressions of policy by the Senate. The Chairman of the Budget Review Committee or his designee may sit with the appropriate committee of the administration when it formulates its budget policy guidelines for the coming year and when categories of the budget are discussed or adopted. The Budget Review Committee shall report its activities to the Senate and shall bring to its attention any instance of non-compliance of the budget with the existing priorities or policies and any other allocations which, in the Committee's opinion, are not in the best interests of the University.

4. Committee on Physical Development of the University

The Committee on Physical Development of the University shall consist of 16 members apportioned as follows: 5 tenured faculty, 2 non-tenured faculty, 2 administrators, 3 students, 1 alumnus, 1 library staff, 1 research staff, and 1 administrative staff.

The primary mandate of the Physical Development Committee is to satisfy itself that the processes for planning, reviewing, assigning priorities and implementing the University's physical development operate effectively. In addition, the Committee will work with the administration and appropriate committees of the Trustees in reviewing, with respect to the University's academic goals, the long-term physical development plans of the University, for the campus and for off-campus properties, and the effects of those plans on the community. The Committee shall meet periodically with the appropriate vice president and his or her designates to discuss the status of planned and ongoing major capital improvements for the University. In addition, the Committee shall regularly receive reports from pertinent departments and committees charged with academically relevant aspects of physical development. The Committee may also advise the administration and the Trustees on faculty, student and staff concerns, priorities and particular projects related to physical development. The Committee on Physical Development shall work closely with the Committee on Education so that developmental plans may bear close relationship to the fulfillment of educational policies and purposes. The Committee shall also work closely with the Committee on External Relations to minimize areas of conflict and maximize areas of cooperation with the community. On behalf of the Senate, the Committee shall also serve as a forum for reviewing reports of exceptional difficulties experienced with the academic physical plant, buildings, grounds and maintenance.

5. Committee on Faculty Affairs, Academic Freedom and Tenure

The Committee on Faculty Affairs, Academic Freedom and Tenure shall consist of 17 members, of whom 13 shall be tenured faculty and 4 non-tenured faculty. One of its members shall also be a member of the Committee on Rules of University Conduct. It shall have jurisdiction of all matters relating to terms and conditions of academic employment including, but not limited to, tenure and academic freedom, academic advancement, sabbatical and other leaves, faculty conduct and discipline, retirement, faculty housing and other faculty prerequisites. The Committee shall also review and, when appropriate, recommend revision of policies governing the appointment of persons to named chairs.

The Committee on Faculty Affairs, Academic Freedom and Tenure, or one of its subcommittees shall also sit as board of appeal on faculty grievances. When acting in such judicial capacity the Committee, or its subcommittee, shall function in a confidential manner and shall not be required to report its deliberations to the Senate as a whole. With the consent, or at the request of the petitioner, however, the Committee or its subcommittee may make public its recommendations and reasons there for.

6. Committee on Student Affairs

The Committee on Student Affairs shall consist of all 22 student Senators and all student non-Senator observers from affiliated institutions, including two from Teachers College and one from Union Theological Seminary. One of its members shall also be a member of the Committee on Rules of University Conduct. Its jurisdiction shall cover matters of student life including, but not limited to, student organizations, student housing, extracurricular activities and student concerns in the community. The Committee's jurisdiction, however, is restricted to matters of University-wide student concerns, and to concerns of students in more than one faculty or school. Where student interests are closely related to the interests of other groups in the University, the Committee shall cooperate with other appropriate committees of the Senate.

7.Committee on External Relations and Research Policy

The Committee on External Relations and Research Policy shall consist of 18 members apportioned as follows: 7 tenured faculty, 2 non-tenured faculty, 3 students, 2 administrators, 1 library staff, 1 alumnus, 2 research staff. The Committee shall review and recommend policies for the University's external relations involving instruction, research, and public affairs, including community relations. The Committee's purview will include the University's research strategies and its relations with private and public sponsoring agencies, as well as the University's strategies for enhancing its local, national, and international reputation through its connections with other academic institutions, governmental agencies, the media, and the surrounding community. The Committee shall meet periodically with the Vice President for Public Affairs and his designates.

8.Committee on Rules of University Conduct

The Committee on Rules of University Conduct shall consist of 15 members apportioned as follows: 4 tenured faculty, 2 non-tenured faculty, 5 students, 2 administrators, 1 library staff, and 1 administrative staff. One of its members shall also be a member of the Committee on Faculty Affairs, Academic Freedom and Tenure, and one shall also be a member of the Student Affairs Committee. It shall have jurisdiction to review and recommend revision of rules of University conduct, as well as the means of enforcing those rules. In matters pertaining to rules of conduct and tribunals for faculty, the Rules Committee shall consult with the Faculty Affairs Committee, and in matters pertaining to such rules and tribunals for students, it shall consult with the Student Affairs Committee. The Committee shall, to the extent appropriate, incorporate its proposals in the form of amendments to the University Statutes and shall submit the same to the University Senate as a whole, to become effective upon adoption by the Senate with the concurrence of the Trustees. [See the Columbia University Charters and Statutes, amended June 7, 1999, chapter XLI, Rules of University Conduct.]

9. Committee on Alumni Relations

The Committee on Alumni Relations shall consist of six members apportioned as follows: 1 tenured faculty, 1 non-tenured faculty, 1 student, 1 administrator, and 2 alumni. The Committee shall encourage more effective communication with alumni. The Committee shall stimulate alumni loyalty and support for the University and shall serve as liaison between the University Senate and various alumni groups. The Committee shall work with the administration in the furtherance of these purposes.

10. Committee on Honors and Prizes

The Committee on Honors and Prizes shall consist of 15 members apportioned as follows: 6 tenured faculty, 2 non-tenured faculty, 2 students, 2 administrators, 1 library staff, 1 research staff and 1 alumnus. The Committee on Honors and Prizes shall recommend policies relating to the award of University prizes and honors to persons who are not members of the University. The Committee shall consider and report to the Senate standards and policies (not inconsistent with such limitations as may legally bind the University under specific endowments or grants) for the award of honorary degrees, the University Medal for Excellence, the various categories of the Pulitzer Prize and other similar evidences of academic recognition. The Committee shall work with the President and the Trustees in the selection of recipients for honorary degrees and prizes. In deliberating on nominations for prizes and honors, the Committee may act in executive session and in confidential manner, and shall not be required to report its deliberations or actions to the Senate as a whole.

11. Committee on Libraries and Academic Computing
    Facilities

The Committee on Libraries and Academic Computing Facilities shall consist of 17 members apportioned as follows: 5 tenured faculty, 2 non-tenured faculty, 3 students, 1 administrator, 2 administrators or administrative staff from the computer center, 2 library staff, 1 research staff, and 1 alumnus. One of its faculty members shall be familiar with the University's computing facilities, and one student member shall be a graduate student and frequent user of the University's computer facilities.

The Committee shall review and recommend University policies relating to the libraries and computer facilities in support of the University's educational purposes. The Committee shall review both short- and long-term policies relating to the operation of the University bookstore and offer suggestions for improvements. The Committee shall work with the libraries, computer facilities, and the University bookstores, as well as the President and the Trustees to implement such policies.

12. Committee on Senate Structure and Operations

The Committee on Senate Structure and Operations shall consist of 12 members apportioned as follows: 6 tenured faculty, 1 non-tenured faculty, 2 students, 2 administrators, and 1 administrative staff. The Committee shall observe and review the operations and effectiveness of the University Senate and make recommendations for the improvement of the structure and operations of the Senate, through statutory amendment and otherwise. The Committee shall be the University Senate's committee on the Senate's rules and procedures.

UNIVERSITY STATUTES
CHAPTER II: THE UNIVERSITY SENATE

ß20. MEMBERSHIP. The University Senate shall be a unicameral body whose membership shall be composed of representatives from the following categories:

a. Administration Members:
    1. The President
    2. The Provost (or if there is more than one Provost, the Provost designated by the President)
    3. The Dean of the Faculty of the Graduate School of Arts and Sciences

4. The Dean of Columbia College
5. Five members who shall be appointed by the President from among officers of administration who are part of the central administration and administrators of Faculties

b. Faculty Members:
   1. Forty-two officers of instruction having an appointment without stated term as professor or associate professor as defined in Sections 60 and 61 to be elected from and by such officers of instruction, subject to the provisions of Section 21.
   2. Fifteen officers of instruction having an appointment for stated term as defined in Sections 60 and 61 to be elected from and by such officers of instruction, subject to the provisions of Section 21.

c. Student Members:
   Twenty-one students as defined in Section 351 to be elected from and by such students as provided in Section 21, and one student from Barnard College to be elected from and by the students of Barnard college as provided in Section 21.

d. Affiliated Institution Members:
   1. Two representatives of the Faculty of Barnard College
   2. Subject to renegotiation of the existing affiliation agreement with Teachers College, two representatives of the Faculty of Teachers College.
   3. Subject to renegotiation of the existing affiliation agreement with the Union Theological Seminary, one representative of the faculty of the Union Theological Seminary.

e. Professional Library Staff:
   Two members who shall be elected from and by those persons holding a full-time Trustee or Presidential appointment to the professional library service.

f. Research Members:

Two members who shall be elected from and by those persons designated as senior research scientist or senior research scholar, research scientist or research scholar, associate research scientist or associate research scholar, post-doctoral research scientist or post-doctoral research scholar, senior staff associate and staff associate, as defined in Section 62 of these Statutes, and who are not entitled to vote as officers of instruction.

g. Administrative Staff Members:

Two members who shall be elected from and by those persons having an appointment from the President or the Secretary of the University or who are in grade VII or above of the University Personnel Classification System for Officers of Administration and Supporting Staff and who are not entitled to vote in any other category for members of the University Senate.

h. Alumni Members:

Two alumni members who shall be chosen by the Alumni Council of the Alumni Federation of the University.

ß21. ELECTIONS, ELIGIBILITY, RECALL AND TERM OF OFFICE.

a. Election of Faculty Members:

1. The forty-two memberships for officers of instruction having an appointment without stated term as professor or associate professor as defined in Sections 60 and 61 shall be apportioned by the University Senate biennially among the Faculties of the Columbia Corporation in proportion to their number of such officers of instruction; provided, however, that each such Faculty, other than the Faculty of Arts and Sciences which shall not be entitled to elect any members, shall be entitled to elect at least one member; no such Faculty shall elect more than five members; the Faculty of International and Public Affairs shall elect only one member; and for the purposes of this sub-section (1), the Faculty of the Graduate School of Arts and Sciences shall be

treated as consisting of three separate Faculties comprising the members of the Faculty appointed to the departments within the Social Sciences, Humanities, and Pure Sciences, respectively, as specified in Section 153 of the Statutes; and the Faculty of the Graduate School of Arts and Sciences may elect to apportion its members among the several departments within the Faculty as it shall determine.

2. The fifteen memberships for officers of instruction with stated term shall be apportioned by the University Senate biennially among the Faculties of the Columbia Corporation other than the Faculty of Arts and Sciences. All officers of instruction having an appointment as preceptor, associate, lecturer, instructor and assistant professor, regardless of whether all such officers are full-time or part-time, shall be entitled to vote. Officers of instruction having an appointment with stated term above that of assistant professor shall also be entitled to vote in this category. For the purposes of this sub-section (2), the Faculty of the Graduate School of Arts and Sciences shall be treated as consisting of three separate Faculties comprised of the departments within the Social Sciences, Humanities, and Pure Sciences, respectively, as specified in Section 153 of the Statutes.

b. Election of Student Members:

The twenty-two memberships for students shall be apportioned by the University Senate biennially as follows: Twenty-one among the Faculties of the Columbia Corporation; provided, however, that at least one student member shall be elected from each Faculty; two additional student members shall be elected from the Faculty with the largest number of full-time students; one additional student member shall be elected from each of the Faculties with the next largest number of students, until the limit of twenty-one students for the Columbia Corporation is reached; and one student member shall be elected from Barnard College. For the purposes of this sub-paragraph (b), the Faculty of Medicine shall be treated as consisting of two separate Faculties, one such Faculty to consist of the program in Medicine, and one such Faculty to consist of the programs in Public Health, Nursing, Occupational Therapy, and Physical Therapy. For the purposes of this sub-paragraph (b), the Faculty of the Graduate School of Arts and Sciences shall be treated as consisting of three separate Faculties comprised of the departments within the Social Sciences, Humanities, and Pure Sciences, respectively, as specified in Section 153 of the Statutes.

c. Election of Members from Professional Library Staff, Research Staff, and Administrative Staff:
     Two members shall be elected from and by the research staff, library staff and administrative staff.

d. Representatives from Affiliated Institutions:
     Each of the affiliated institutions shall choose representatives from among their respective Faculties to serve as members in such manner as each of them may determine.

e. Direct and Indirect Election:
     All members elected under sub-paragraphs (a), (b), and (c) shall be chosen by direct election, except that student members may be chosen by indirect election as hereinafter provided. If the indirect election method is chosen, then the student member of the University Senate shall be elected by the elected student governing body of the Faculty from which the student member of the University Senate is being chosen. Such choice shall be exercised only by a referendum of the students within such Faculty and shall stand unless and until reversed by a succeeding referendum. If there is no elected student governing body of the Faculty which is authorized to hold indirect elections, and if either seat assigned to a student member has remained vacant for six months or longer, or elections have failed to fill such a seat, then a member may be elected from one or more departments within that Faculty in rotation, as may be prescribed by the body designated of the University Senate, to administer University Senate elections.

f. Time of Election and Term of Office:

There shall be two regular election periods each year, one in the spring and one in the fall. The regular term of office for each member shall be as follows: (1) For each member elected in the spring elections, the term of office shall begin fourteen days before the day of Commencement next following his or her election and shall be for two years; provided that a member elected to a vacant seat shall assume office immediately; and provided further that if the spring elections are not completed by the date set for the beginning of his or her term, the member shall assume office immediately upon the completion of the elections; (2) for each member elected in the fall elections, the term of office shall commence immediately upon election and shall expire fourteen days before the day of second Commencement next following his or her election; (3) for each appointed member the term of office shall commence immediately upon appointment and shall expire fourteen days before the day of the second Commencement next following his or her appointment. It shall be the responsibility of each member to advise the commission supervising elections of members to the University Senate, as early as possible, if he or she will be unable to serve his or her full term. When such commission is so advised, provision will be made to vote, at the next election, for a member to fill the anticipated vacancy. The term of such member shall be the same as that of all other members elected in the same election period, except that if the seat is occupied at the time of election, the term shall commence upon the effective date of resignation of the retiring member. Except as provided in sub-paragraph (f), any vacancy occurring between election periods shall be filled in the same manner in which the original member was chosen, and the term of office for each member so elected shall commence immediately upon election and shall expire fourteen days before the day of the second Commencement next following the election. The Executive Committee of the University Senate may designate a day for the expiration of terms and beginnings of new terms different from the date set herein, if such a re-designation is necessary to allow for an orderly transition of the work of the University Senate from one session to the next. No person shall be disqualified from election because he or she will be a member of the category from which he or she is elected for less than two years. However, his or her membership shall terminate when he or she is no longer a member of the category from which he or she was elected.

g. Recall:
Every elected member shall be subject to recall. Upon petition signed by one-fourth of the number of members of the category from which the member was elected, a recall election shall be held. A majority of votes cast for recall shall cause the recall of the member and his membership shall thereupon become vacant. The provisions of sub-paragraph (f) shall also apply to recall elections.

ß22. DUTIES. It shall be the duty of the University Senate:

a. to report to the Trustees its opinion as to any exercise of power proposed by a Faculty under Section 35;
b. to submit such proposals to the Trustees or to the President or to the several Faculties as in its judgment may serve to increase the efficiency of University work;
c. to consider any questions that may arise as to the conduct or efficiency of any officer of administration or instruction, and to report thereon to the Trustees through the President.

ß23. GENERAL POLICIES. Subject to the reserve power of the Trustees and the provisions of Section 25, the University Senate shall be a policy-making body which may consider all matters of University-wide concern, all matters affecting more than one Faculty or School, and all matters pertaining to the implementation and execution of agreements with the other educational institutions that are now or may hereafter become affiliated with the University. Without limitation by enumeration the University Senate shall:

a. develop and review plans and policies to strengthen the educational system of the University;
b. work on the long-range master plan for the physical development of the University; recommend ways in which it can be improved; and keep the same under continuing review;

c. work for the advancement of academic freedom and the protection of faculty interests;
d. work for the promotion of student welfare and the enhancement of student life;
e. initiate and review policies to govern the University's relations with outside agencies for research, instruction and related purposes;
f. foster policies for cooperative and mutually beneficial relations with the neighboring community;
g. review by broad categories the annual budget of the University after its adoption and advise the Trustees as to its general conformity with the goals of the University;
h. consider and recommend policies relating to the awarding of University prizes and honors, and assist the Trustees in the selection of recipients of such prizes and honors;
i. promulgate a code of conduct for faculty, students and staff and provide for its enforcement;
j. initiate proposed changes in Chapter II of these Statutes which have been passed by a vote of at least three-fifths of all incumbent members of the University Senate.

ß24. POWERS. The University Senate, subject to the reserved power of the Trustees and the provisions of Section 25, shall have power, and it shall be its duty:

a. Academic Correlation: to secure the correlation of courses offered by the several Faculties and Administrative Boards; to adjust all questions involving more than one Faculty or Administrative Board.
b. Degrees: to prescribe, by concurrent action with the appropriate Faculty or Administrative Board, the conditions upon which the following degrees shall be conferred, and to recommend candidates for such degrees:

Doctor of Philosophy (Ph.D.)   Faculty of the Graduate
                                            School   of Arts and
                                            Sciences and
                                            Administrative Board of

	the Graduate School of Arts and Sciences
Doctor of the Science of Law (J.S.D.)	Faculty of Law
Doctor of Medical Sciences (Med.Sc.D.)	Faculty of Medicine
Doctor of Public Health (Dr. P.H.) Faculty of Medicine	
Doctor of Education (Ed.D.)	Faculty of Teachers College
Doctor of Enginering Sciences	Faculty of Engineering and Applied Science
Doctor of Social Welfare (D.S.W.)	Faculty of Social Work
Doctor of Library Service	Faculty of Library Service
Master of Architecture (M. Arch.)	Faculty of Architecture, Planning, and Preservation
Master of Philosophy (M. Phil.)	Faculty of the Graduate School of Arts and Sciences and Administrative Board of the Graduate School of Arts and Sciences
Master of Arts (M.A.)	Faculties of the Graduate School of Arts and Sciences
Master of Science (M.S.)	Faculties of Medicine, Engineering and Applied Science, Teachers College, Architecture, Planning, and Preservation, Journalism, Library Service, Dental and Oral Surgery, Social Work, and Business
Master of Business Administration (M.B.A.)	Faculty of Business
Master of International Affairs (M.I.A.)	Faculty of International and Public Affairs
Master of Laws (LL.M.)	Faculty of Law
Master of Public Administration (M.P.A.)	Faculty of International and Public Affairs

Master of Fine Arts (M.F.A.)	Faculty of the Arts
Master of Public Health (M.P.H.)	Faculty of Medicine
Master of Comparative Law (M.C.L.)	Faculty of Law
Master of Education (Ed.M.)	Faculty of Teachers College
Bachelor of Science (B.S.)	Faculty of Teachers College, Engineering and Applied Science
Master of Arts in Teaching (M.A.T.)	Faculty of Teachers College
Doctor of Musical Arts (D.M.A.)	Faculty of Arts
Master of Arts in Liberal Studies	Faculty of General Studies

c.   Certificates. To prescribe the conditions upon which the fol-
     lowing certificates, and such other certificates as the Univer-
     sity Senate may from time to time approve, shall be awarded
     upon recommendation of the several Faculties, Administra-
     tive Boards, or Committees:

Certificate in Dentistry	Faculty of Dental and Oral Surgery
Certificate in Advanced General Education	Faculty of Dental and Oral Surgery in Dentistry
Certificate in Occupational Therapy	Faculty of Medicine
Certificate in Physical Therapy	Faculty of Medicine
Certificate in Psychoanalytic Training	Faculty of Medicine
Certificate in Maternity Nursing	Faculty of Medicine
Certificate in Critical Care	Faculty of Medicine
Certificate in Nurse Anesthesia	Faculty of Medicine
Certificate in Nurse Midwifery	Faculty of Medicine
Certificate in Oncology	Faculty of Medicine
Certificate in Primary Care—Adult	Faculty of Medicine
Certificate in Primary Care—Family	Faculty of Medicine
Certificate in Primary Care—Geriatric	Faculty of Medicine
Certificate in Primary Care—Neonatal	Faculty of Medicine
Certificate in Primary Care—Pediatric	Faculty of Medicine
Certificate in Psychiatric/Mental Health	Faculty of Medicine
Professional Certificate in Social Work	Faculty of Social Work

Certificate of East Asian Institute	Administrative, Committee, East Asian Institute
Certificate of Institute on Western Europe	Administrative Committee, Institute on Western Europe
Certificate of the Harriman Institute	Administrative Committee, the Harriman Institute
Certificate of Middle East Institute	Administrative Committee, the Middle East Institute
Certificate of Institute of Latin American	Administrative Committee, Institute of Latin and Iberian Studies and Iberian Studies
Certificate in Accounting	Faculty of General Studies
Certificate of Program in East Central	Coordinating Committee, Program on East European Studies Central European Studies
Certificate in Advanced International	Faculty of Journalism Reporting
Certificate in Advanced Science Writing	Faculty of Journalism
Certificate in Advanced Librarianship	Faculty of Library Service
Certificate in Library and Archives	Faculty of Library Service Conservation
Teachers College Professional Diploma	Faculty of Teachers College
Certificate for Postdoctoral Respecialization	Faculty of Teachers College
Certificate in Advanced Social Welfare	Faculty of Social Work
Certificate in Medieval and Renaissance	Faculty of the Graduate School Studies of Arts and Sciences

d. College Courses: to prescribe, by concurrent action with the Faculties of Columbia College, Barnard College and General Studies, severally, the extent to which courses offered by other Faculties and leading to graduate or professional degrees, or diplomas shall be included in the programs of studies under those Faculties, and the conditions upon which such courses may be elected by candidates for a nonprofessional first degree;

e. Barnard College: to prescribe the manner in which the degree of Bachelor of Arts conferred upon graduates of Barnard College shall be maintained at all times as a degree of equal value with the degree of Bachelor of Arts conferred upon the graduates of Columbia College;

f. Other Institutions: to adopt regulations, subject to approval by the Trustees, providing for the proper execution, as regards educational matters, of agreements that are now in existence or that may hereafter be made between the University and such other educational institutions as are now or may hereafter become affiliated with the University, and prescribe what degrees, diplomas, and certificates may be granted by said institutions and the conditions for granting the same;

g. Summer Session: to adopt regulations governing the relation of instruction in the Summer Session to the other work of the University;

h. Fellowships and Scholarships: to determine the conditions upon which fellowships and University scholarships shall be awarded, to appoint all fellows and university scholars, and to make rules for their government, subject to such restrictions as may be prescribed by the Statutes or by the terms upon which the several fellowships and university scholarships are established;

i. Academic Calendar: to fix, annually in advance the Academic Calendar, the dates for entrance and final examinations, the date of Commencement, and the order of Commencement exercises;

j. Research Bureaus: to encourage original research and to authorize the establishment of research bureaus to be conducted by a faculty or by one or more departments under such terms as the University Senate may prescribe.

k. Libraries: to advise in such matters pertaining to the administration of the libraries as may be laid before it by the Provost or Provosts or by the University Librarian.

ß25. LIMITATIONS OF POWERS.

a. Unless Trustee concurrence is required, acts of the University Senate under Sections 22 and 23 shall become final on passage. In all matters involving a change in budgetary appropriations; involving the acquisition or disposition of real property; affecting contractual obligations of the University; or as required by law, such concurrence shall be required. In all other matters, the action of the University Senate will be final unless the President shall advise the University Senate not later than its next regularly scheduled meeting that Trustee concurrence is necessary. Acts of the University Senate under Sections 22 and 23 shall be concurred in or not concurred in by the Trustees by the second stated meeting of the Trustees following the submission of the University Senate's action to the Trustees, except when the Trustees shall advise the University Senate of their need for a longer specified period of time to consider such actions. Whenever the Trustees do not concur in any act of the University Senate under Sections 22 and 23, they shall return the measure to the University Senate with an explanation of the reason for their action.

b. No exercise of the powers conferred on the University Senate by Section 24 which involves a change in the educational policy of the University in respect to the requirements of admission or the conditions of graduation shall take effect until the same shall have been submitted to the Trustees at one meeting and another meeting of the Trustees shall have been held.

c. Notwithstanding the provisions of sub-sections (a) and (b), the President may convene a special meeting of the University Senate within 15 class days of any University Senate action, and may request it to reconsider such action.

ß26. BY-LAWS AND COMMITTEES. The University Senate shall have the power to organize itself and to make all such By-Laws and regulations for its own proceedings as shall not contravene the Charter of the University or these Statutes. Such By-Laws shall be amended only by a three-fifths vote of all incumbent members of the University Senate. Any such By-

Laws and regulations may provide for such committees as may be necessary or desirable. Such committees shall include an Executive Committee. The Executive Committee of the Trustees shall work with the Exectutive Committee of the University Senate in the nomination of six Trustees as provided by the By-Laws of the Trustees. The Executive Committee of the Trustees shall work with the Executive Committee of the University Senate in the selection of a President of the University as provided in the By-Laws of the Trustees. The President shall work with the Executive Committee of the University Senate in the selection of the Provost or Provosts as provided in Section 50. The Executive Committee of the University Senate shall participate in the appointment of University professors as provided in Section 61.

ß27. MEETINGS. The University Senate shall meet regularly as provided in its By-Laws. Special meetings shall be held on the call of the President and in accordance with its By-Laws. The President shall be the presiding officer of the University Senate. In the absence of the President, the Chairman of the Executive Committee of the University Senate shall preside.

ß28. STAFF. The University shall furnish, to the extent provided for in the University's budget, assistance to the University Senate as a whole and to its committees in connection with its official business, as may be authorized by the Executive Committee of the University Senate.

RULES OF PROCEDURE OF THE UNIVERSITY SENATE

The Columbia University Senate is governed by the current edition of Robert's Rules of Order and, in addition, by those rules appearing below which have a particular application to this body.

RULE 1
MEETING TIME. Meetings of the Senate shall be convened at 1:15 p.m. and adjourned at 5:00 p.m. Prior to 5 p.m., the Chairman may entertain a motion for adjournment or for an extension of time.

Unfinished business shall be held over until, and placed on the agenda for, the next regular or special meeting of the Senate.

RULE 2
WRITTEN RESOLUTIONS. Members making proposals or amendments on the floor shall immediately transmit them in writing to the President.

RULE 3
COMMUNICATION WITH NON-SENATORS. Only members of the Senate and those persons specified in Section 1 (g) of the By-Laws may address the Senate when it is in session. Other persons wishing to communicate with the entire body of the Senate may do so in writing, and the Secretariat shall distribute such written communication to all Senators provided that 125 copies are deposited with it at least 24 hours prior to any particular session. On extraordinary occasions, the Senate may, by a two-thirds vote taken at any session, schedule a convocation of the Senate to hear persons who wish to address it or whom the Senate wishes to invite to address it. At such convocation no business shall be transacted and no motion or vote shall be in order. Upon recommendation of the Executive Committee, the Senate may decide, by a two-thirds vote, to hear speakers not covered in the above provision.

RULE 4
RECORD VOTE. By a one-third vote of the members present and voting, a written and signed ballot may be taken on substantive questions. Tellers will make an immediate count of the votes, and after the result has been announced, the Secretariat will proceed to register the individual members' votes for release at the end of the meeting.

RULE 5
UNANIMOUS CONSENT. When the Committee on Education reports to the Senate concerning minor changes in degree requirements or degree-granting programs, it may ask that such resolutions adopted by unanimous consent. Copies of these resolutions must have been circulated in advance to all members

of the Senate and to the deans of all divisions of the University. If, at the conclusion of the reading of the relevant resolution or at any other time within 30 days following the sending out of such information, no objection has been made by any senator, the recommendations of the Committee on Education shall be regarded as having been formally adopted at the close of the second plenary meeting following the original report.

RULE 6

SUSPENSION OF THE RULES. A motion to suspend the rules, if there is objection, shall not pass except by a three-fifths vote of all incumbent members of the Senate.